NORTHERN LIGHTS

A PRACTICAL TRAVEL GUIDE

POLLY EVANS

www.bradtguides.com

Bradt Guides Ltd, UK
The Globe Pequot Press Inc, USA

Bradt GUIDES
TRAVEL TAKEN SERIOUSLY

AUTHOR

Polly Evans is an award-winning journalist and writer. She's the author of Bradt's *Yukon*, as well as five narrative travel books, the most recent of which, *Mad Dogs and an Englishwoman*, tells the story of her learning to drive sled dogs in northern Canada. When not on the road, Polly lives in Berkshire.

Fourth edition published March 2023
First published 2010
Bradt Guides Ltd
31a High Street, Chesham, Buckinghamshire, HP5 1BW, England
www.bradtguides.com
Print edition published in the USA by The Globe Pequot Press Inc,
PO Box 480, Guilford, Connecticut 06437-0480

Project Manager: Laura Pidgley
Cover research: Ian Spick, Bradt Guides

ISBN: 9781804690598

British Library Cataloguing in Publication Data
A catalogue record for this book is available from the British Library

Photographs © individual photographers and tourist organisations credited beside images and also those from picture libraries credited as follows: Alamy.com (A); Shutterstock.com (S); Superstock.com (SS)
Front cover Aurora borealis over the Lofoten Islands, Norway (Piotr Krzeslak/S)
Back cover Dog sledding in northern Iceland (Visit North Iceland); Hotel Nangu (Wilderness Hotels Mediabank)
Title page The northern lights over Finland (Antti Pietikäinen/Visit Finland); Ski touring in northern Norway (Kristin Folsland Olsen/Visit Norway); Reindeer ride in Lapland (Juho Kuva/Visit Finland)
Maps David McCutcheon FBCart.S

Typeset by Ian Spick, Bradt Guides
Production managed by Zenith Media; printed in the UK
Digital conversion by www.dataworks.co.in

Contents

LIST OF MAPS

The northern lights dancing in Finland

THOMAS KAST/VISIT FINLAND

Introduction

One night several years ago, I went on an evening visit to a commercial northern lights viewing centre in Yellowknife, in Canada's Northwest Territories. I didn't much want to go. I'd spent several months living in the far north, researching a book about dog sledding, and I'd seen the northern lights plenty of times. I'd become a bit blasé about tourist outings given that I'd watched the aurora regularly from the comfort of my own cabin. That evening, I preferred the idea of curling up beneath the duvet and going to sleep. But I was working as a journalist, specialising in the Arctic and sub-Arctic, and I had to.

And so began one of the most remarkable evenings of my life. That night, the northern lights put on the most extraordinary display, the likes of which I had never imagined. First, they crept up like green bony fingers from the horizon, as I'd seen many times before. But then they grew and swirled until they swept across the entire sky. They seemed to take on every possible form. At times they unfurled from the horizon like a flower at dawn. Then they'd stretch out into an arched streamer, and undulate like a flag flapping in the breeze. At times they seemed to climb up into a three-dimensional tepee which collapsed downwards like a pile of luminous pick-up-sticks. The aurora was pale green with a scarlet underbelly, and it danced across the starry black sky with a speed I'd never thought possible.

I'd climbed to the top of a small hill, set up my tripod, and begun to take photographs. The pictures were beyond my photographic dreams – but I could only snap one segment of sky, then another, and I couldn't record the wild energy of the aurora as it tumbled across the sky. And so I stopped pressing the button. Instead, I lay down on my back in the snow, and allowed myself to be consumed by the show overhead. It lasted just 10 or 15 minutes but provided perhaps the most intense experience of beauty that I have ever known.

Many people travelling in quest of the northern lights won't catch a display of this level. Some won't manage to make their visit coincide with any auroral activity at all. But even if you're unlucky with the lights, a trip to the Arctic in winter will provide memories that, in my opinion, outstrip any beach holiday. There's something about the blue light of the mornings that turns buttercup yellow at noon, then takes on pinky tinges as evening falls, the serenity of the pure white landscapes, the impossibly intricate design of a single snowflake, the sparkling jewels of hoar frost that grow on the branches of spruce, that never ceases to entrance. In the daytime, there's dog sledding, skiing and snowshoeing for the energetic, and snowmobiling for adrenalin enthusiasts; as for the night, the far north is home to an ever-increasing array of ice hotels, ultra-chic igloos, and cosy log cabins with roaring wood stoves. I hope this book will help you to learn a little not just about the northern lights, but also about the wider experience the northern countries offer. And I hope that you, like me, will find your Arctic journey so mesmerising that, across the years, you can't help but return.

FEEDBACK REQUEST

At Bradt Guides we're aware that guidebooks start to go out of date on the day they're published – and that you, our readers, are out there in the field doing research of your own. You'll find out before us when a fine new family-run hotel opens or a favourite restaurant changes hands and goes downhill. So why not tell us about your experiences? Contact us on 01753 893444 or e info@bradtguides.com. We will forward emails to the author who may post updates on the Bradt website at w bradtguides.com/updates. Alternatively, you can add a review of the book to Amazon, or share your adventures with us on Facebook, Twitter or Instagram (@BradtGuides).

1

What Are the Northern Lights?

The ancient Greenlanders thought the northern lights were a sign from the heavens that their ancestors were trying to contact the living. The Norwegians saw them as old maids dancing. Modern science is rather more prosaic. It tells us that the northern lights are created by charged solar

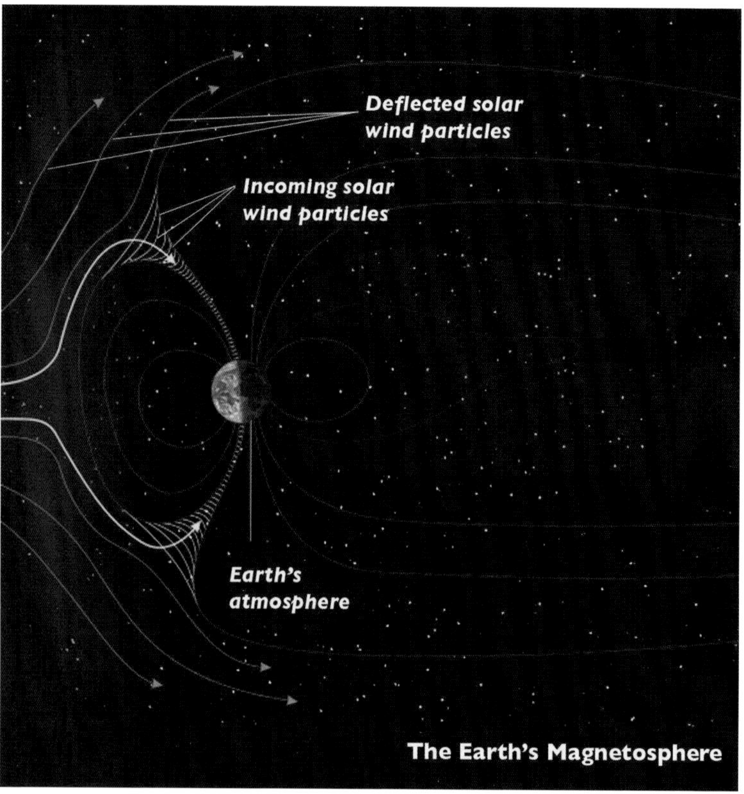

The Earth's Magnetosphere

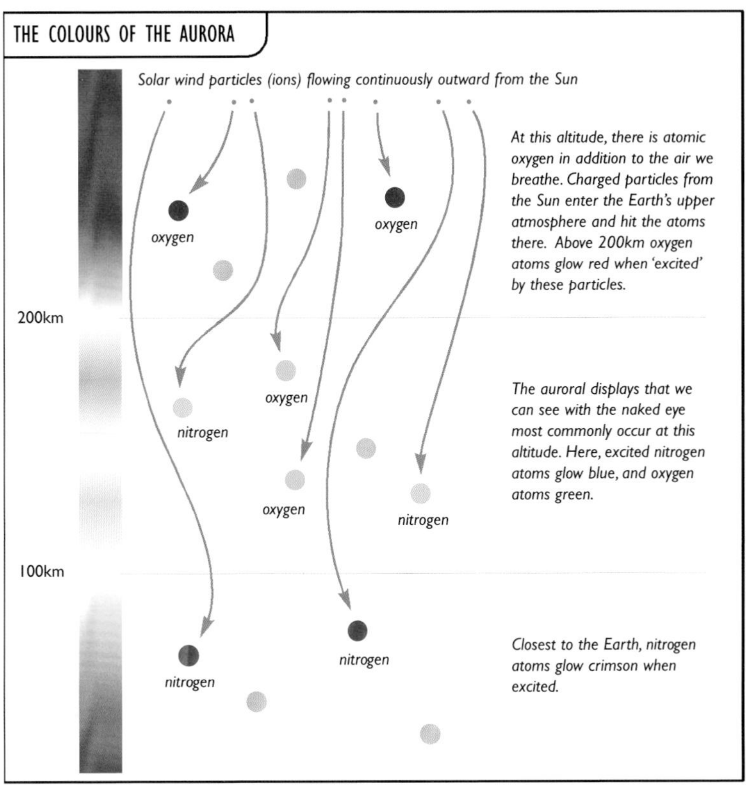

THE COLOURS OF THE AURORA
Solar wind particles (ions) flowing continuously outward from the Sun
oxygen
oxygen
At this altitude, there is atomic oxygen in addition to the air we breathe. Charged particles from the Sun enter the Earth's upper atmosphere and hit the atoms there. Above 200km oxygen atoms glow red when 'excited' by these particles.
200km
oxygen
nitrogen
The auroral displays that we can see with the naked eye most commonly occur at this altitude. Here, excited nitrogen atoms glow blue, and oxygen atoms green.
oxygen
nitrogen
100km
nitrogen
nitrogen
Closest to the Earth, nitrogen atoms glow crimson when excited.

particles ejected from the Sun in a solar wind during explosions or flares. If these particles reach the Earth – a journey that takes two or three days – they are diverted around the planet by the Earth's magnetic fields. (If they were allowed to penetrate the Earth's atmosphere, they would damage us with their intense radiation.)

Most of the solar wind travels around the Earth and disappears into space. Some particles, however, enter the Earth's upper atmosphere at its polar regions. As they do so, they collide with atoms and molecules there, which absorb some of the solar particles' energy. This is referred to as 'exciting' the atom or molecule. In order to return to their normal state, the atoms and molecules emit photons, or light particles. The northern lights are therefore an actual source of light, not a reflection of sunlight as some people suppose.

The colour of the northern lights depends on which gas the solar particles collide with. In the auroral displays that are most commonly to be seen

1

PINKY/S

2

HANS PETTER SØRENSEN/FAROUTFOCUS/VISIT NORWAY

WHAT DOES 'AURORA BOREALIS' MEAN?

Literally, aurora borealis translates from the Latin as 'northern dawn'. There's some dispute as to who first coined the expression. Some attribute it to Italian scientist Galileo Galilei who saw the major aurora of 12 September 1621 (page 88); others claim French astronomer Pierre Gassendi first used the phrase following the same event. Either way, the reference to dawn alludes to the red colour that is seen in the aurora at the lower latitudes at which both men would have observed this impressive display.

The southern lights (page 35) are sometimes referred to by their Latin name 'aurora australis'. Together, the northern and southern lights can be called the 'aurora polaris'.

with the naked eye, oxygen emits a greenish-yellow burst of light, while the photons produced by nitrogen are crimson. This activity takes place in the Earth's high atmosphere, at 100km or more above the planet's surface.

MAGNETIC VERSUS GEOGRAPHIC POLES

The Earth's magnetic field lines, which help to create the northern lights by diverting solar particles towards the poles, run between its magnetic rather than geographic poles. So, while the geographic North Pole sits permanently at 90° latitude, and is the point at which all the lines of longitude converge, the Earth's magnetic North Pole – the point towards which your compass needle will swing – moves. This is because it is influenced by the perpetually shifting molten iron that makes up the Earth's outer core. The magnetic North Pole was previously located in the Canadian Arctic, but has in the last few years drifted over the top of the Earth and is now heading towards Siberia.

THE AURORAL OVALS

The convergence of the Earth's magnetic fields around the magnetic North and South poles leads the northern lights to exhibit in auroral ovals, or rings around the top and bottom of the Earth. If you want to see the northern lights, you therefore have to be beneath, or within sight of, the auroral oval. The auroral ovals stay in a fairly fixed location in space while the Earth rotates beneath them. When levels of solar activity are low, the northern auroral oval sits between 60° and 70° of latitude; it is wider on the night-time

◀**1** *The aurora appears red at higher altitudes.* **2** *The aurora over Aldersundet, Norway.*

The auroral oval as seen near Sisimiut, Greenland

MADS PIHL/VISIT GREENLAND

side of the Earth. During a very violent solar flare, however, the auroral oval fattens or bulges and the aurora can be seen from lower latitudes. However fat or thin, the auroral oval is always present but can only be seen in its entirety – as a ring – from space.

So what does the shifting of the magnetic North Pole mean for the aurora? Will it move to Russia? Scientists think not because – wait for it – there's a *third* type of pole. That's the geomagnetic North Pole.

The geomagnetic North Pole is a theoretical entity – you can't pinpoint it on a map. Imagine a massive bar magnet running straight through the Earth's centre. The geomagnetic poles would be the places at either end of the bar magnet where they intersected the Earth's surface. Of course, there is no nice, straight bar magnet because the Earth's core is a chaotically shifting mass of liquid. This theoretical pole, therefore, is the point below which the constantly shifting magnetic fields of our planet start to even out, high up in the stratosphere. Fortunately for aurora spotters, it seems that the aurora is more inclined to stick with the geomagnetic field, so there's no need to strap on your snowshoes and trek across uninhabited Siberia just yet.

THE SUNSPOT CYCLE

Sunspots are dark blotches on the Sun's surface that are cooler than the surrounding regions (though they're not exactly cool – if a sunspot could be suspended in the night sky it would still provide more light than the full moon). Sunspots are temporary phenomena, which contain concentrated magnetic field lines; this intense magnetic activity prevents them heating to the same temperature as the rest of the surface of the Sun. Solar disturbances are greater when sunspot numbers are high – and so, in turn, we see more intense and active northern lights when sunspots are common.

Sunspots come and go in 'sunspot cycles' which peak about every 11 years. During these peaks, solar flares are more common and more energetic, and so the northern lights – though visible at all stages of the sunspot cycle – tend to be more frequent and intense at these times. Additionally, the years following a peak see increased northern lights activity. This is because coronal holes (areas of the Sun that are low in density and have open magnetic fields – the magnetic fields lead out into space rather than looping back into the Sun, and so allow the solar wind to escape from the Sun) form during sunspot cycle peaks, and they too lead to greater auroral activity.

1 & **2** *The aurora manifests in many different shapes and sizes, from undulating ribbons to dazzling rods of colour that burst like a firework.* ▶

1

VESTERÅLEN TOURS

2

DAVID TROOD/VISIT GREENLAND

THE DIFFERENT SHAPES OF THE NORTHERN LIGHTS

The aurora can be seen as undulating ribbons and shimmering curtains, spiky fingers that creep up from the horizon and dazzling rods of colour that burst like a firework from a single point high in the sky. The different shapes are partly caused by the position of the aurora in relation to the magnetic zenith – the point in the sky that you can see if you look along the line of the Earth's magnetic field. If the aurora runs across the observer's magnetic zenith, the observer will see waves or lines converging into a single spot. If the aurora is some distance away from the observer's magnetic zenith, it will look more like a two-dimensional curtain or line. It works a bit like perspective when you stand at the foot of a tall building: looking directly upwards, you see the nearest building's walls converge more sharply than those of buildings some distance away.

CAN YOU HEAR THE NORTHERN LIGHTS?

Indigenous northern people and observers from the lower latitudes have frequently told of hissing, crackling or rustling noises that accompany the aurora. Until recently, scientists couldn't explain this: the northern lights are located in the Earth's upper atmosphere, where the air is too thin to carry sound waves. However, a recent study by scientists at Finland's Aalto University reckons that the solar particles – or the geomagnetic disturbance created by them – generate sound when they're much closer to the ground. Don't expect to hear them during your aurora-watching though. The soundtrack doesn't play alongside every aurora display, and when it does, it is brief and faint. Your best bet for hearing the northern lights is from the comfort of your very own sofa – with an internet search you'll find various websites that claim to have recorded them.

2

Where to See the Northern Lights

It doesn't follow that the further north you travel, the more likely you'll be to see the northern lights. This is because the aurora is most visible beneath the ring known as the auroral oval (page 11), which, though constantly shifting, usually encircles the Earth between 60° and 70° of latitude. You'll therefore have a better chance of seeing the lights dance if you're near the Arctic Circle than if you're at the North Pole.

ALASKA

'The odds are good, but the goods are odd.' So say Alaskan women in search of a man. For many visitors to the USA's frozen north, this is the charm of the place. Here, eccentricity is not only tolerated but celebrated, and men in hard-wearing dungarees guffaw in the face of the southern states' fashionistas.

ALASKA AT A GLANCE

Language English
Population 720,000
Currency US dollar (US$)
Time GMT –9 (summer), –8 (winter)
Electricity 110V; plugs have two flat pins or two flat pins and a round grounding pin

But there's no doubt about it – Alaska's natural world is a dazzler, with mountain ranges, glacier fields and tundra home to moose and caribou, wolves and Arctic foxes. During the winter, daytime activities include dog sledding, snowmobiling and snowshoeing, as well as all manner of skiing experiences including alpine, cross-country, back-country, heli-skiing and snowboarding.

Alaska's economy revolves around the oil and gas, fishing and tourism industries. The former invites a really fascinating tourist experience, with

1 *Alaska's Dalton Highway.* **2** *Caribou roam the wildernesses of Canada and Alaska.* **3** *Takhini Hot Springs, Yukon.* **4** *Ice fishing at Blachford Lake Lodge.* ▶

MOS_RITTIRON/S

STATE OF ALASKA/MICHAEL DEYOUNG

GOVERNMENT OF YUKON/ANDREW STRAIN

MARTINA GEBAROVSKA & BLACHFORD LAKE LODGE

trips to Deadhorse, the community that serves those that work at the Prudhoe Bay oil fields, via the Dalton Highway and Coldfoot Camp.

THE NORTHERN LIGHTS IN ALASKA Of Alaska's towns, **Fairbanks** is the top spot for northern lights viewing thanks to its location beneath the auroral oval; 100km outside town, the lovely Chena Hot Springs resort (page 59) offers aurora viewing either from the hot springs themselves or from the surrounding wilderness.

Having come this far, however, it's worth a little extra travelling into outback Alaska. **Coldfoot Camp** (so named because some gold-rush stampeders got 'cold feet' here and turned around for home) lies 175km north of Fairbanks on the Dalton Highway – a road that cuts through scenery so extraordinary that it's really a destination in itself. But if you're looking for boutique loveliness and a chocolate on your pillow, Coldfoot Camp isn't the spot for you: essentially, it's a truck stop serving the drivers that haul supplies up to the oilfields at Prudhoe Bay. As such, it's full of interesting characters with forests of facial hair. It's not just the people-watching that makes this a fascinating stop for the night, though.

A trip to the nearby village of **Wiseman** (population: five) offers an insight into a world away from cellophane-wrapped joints of meat and evenly shaped vegetables, and the villagers' love and understanding of the land they live in left me, as an urbanite, in genuine awe. Come here in the evening, and they'll conjure up a northern-lights show – weather permitting, of course.

CANADA

Northern Canada is home to some of the world's last wildernesses, where caribou, bears and wolves outnumber human residents. In winter, temperatures dip low, but many insist that this is their favourite time of year: there's an intense beauty to the white silence that reigns across the Canadian north in the snowy months. The auroral oval cuts across the whole of northern Canada, making it a top destination for northern lights tourism; this guide focuses on the western side of the country.

During daylight hours, there's dog sledding, snowmobiling and

CANADA AT A GLANCE

Language English and French
Population 37 million
Currency Canadian dollar (CAN$ or CAD)
Time Time zones vary between GMT–2.5 and GMT–8
Electricity 110V; plugs have two flat pins or two flat pins and a round grounding pin

snowshoeing for outdoors enthusiasts, while Churchill is a top destination for polar bear enthusiasts (page 65).

THE NORTHERN LIGHTS IN CANADA **Yellowknife** is renowned for its northern lights (it's here that I experienced the most spectacular display I've ever seen); excursions include an aurora-viewing evening from a cabin that visitors reach by snowmobiling across Great Slave Lake. For a more remote experience still, fly to the eco-lodge at **Blachford Lake** (page 66) where you can try your hand (and feet) at skating, ice fishing, dog sledding and snowmobiling. Far from artificial light, it's an ideal location for aurora gazing.

Alternatively in Yukon, in **Whitehorse** you can mix your aurora-viewing with dog sledding and sightseeing by air, then lie back in the Takhini Hot Springs and watch the sky turn green while your hair grows white with icicles. In **Churchill**, Manitoba, polar bears pose for photos in the daytime (page 65).

For a truly wild bear-viewing experience, those with advanced wilderness skills can take a helicopter to Yukon's remote **Fishing Branch Ni'iinlii Njik Territorial Park**, where small groups can see the grizzly bears that congregate during the autumn to feed on the spawning salmon – despite sub-zero conditions, water flows here year-round due to thermal energy stored in underground reservoirs. And once the bears have gone to bed, look up to the skies to see if the aurora's coming out to play.

FINLAND

Finland is the most sparsely populated country in the European Union, and the happiest country in the world, according to the United Nations' World Happiness Report. Perhaps the two are linked. Around 25% of its population lives in the cosmopolitan and cultural capital, Helsinki, while the countryside is characterised by its thousands of lakes and islands, and landscapes covered in lush pine, spruce and birch forests. The largest city in Finnish Lapland is **Rovaniemi**, hugely popular with winter tourists for its Santa Claus attractions (page 59), as well as its many museums, restaurants and cafés.

In winter, Finland attracts snow-sports enthusiasts: the country has around 75 ski resorts and tens of

FINLAND AT A GLANCE

Language Finnish
Population 5.5 million
Currency Euro (€)
Time GMT+2 (winter), GMT+3 (summer)
Electricity 220V; plugs have two round pins

In northern Canada, caribou, bears and wolves are said to outnumber human residents.

CHERYL RAMALHO/S

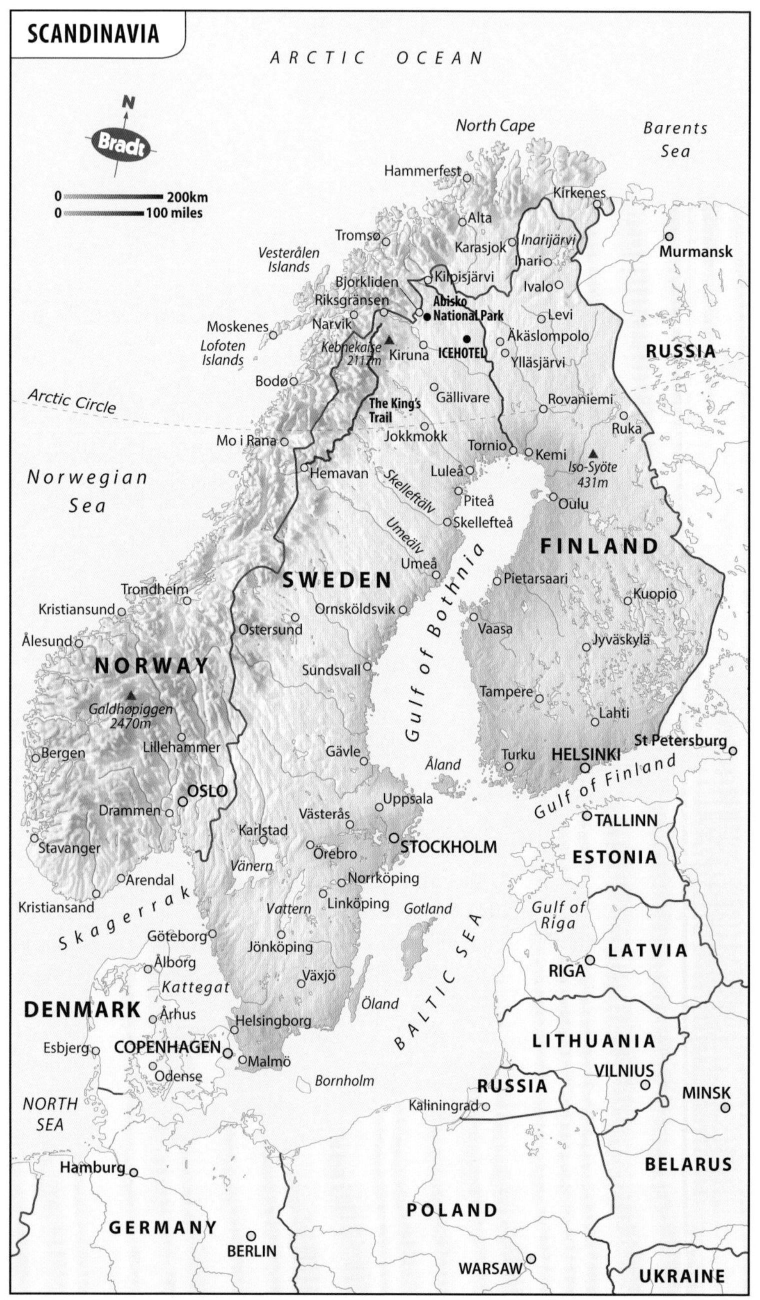
SCANDINAVIA
ARCTIC OCEAN
N
Bradt
0 200km
0 100 miles
North Cape
Barents Sea
Hammerfest
Kirkenes
Alta
Tromsø
Karasjok
Inarijärvi
Inari
Murmansk
Vesterålen Islands
Kilpisjärvi
Bjorkliden
Ivalo
Riksgränsen
Abisko National Park
Levi
Moskenes
Narvik
Äkäslompolo
Lofoten Islands
Kebnekaise 2117m
Kiruna
ICEHOTEL
Ylläsjärvi
RUSSIA
Bodø
Gällivare
Rovaniemi
Arctic Circle
The King's Trail
Ruka
Jokkmokk
Mo i Rana
Tornio
Kemi
Iso-Syöte 431m
Hemavan
Luleå
Norwegian Sea
Skellefteälv
Piteå
Oulu
Skellefteå
Umeälv
FINLAND
Umeå
SWEDEN
Pietarsaari
Trondheim
Kuopio
Kristiansund
Ornsköldsvik
Gulf of Bothnia
Östersund
Vaasa
Ålesund
Jyväskylä
NORWAY
Sundsvall
Galdhøpiggen 2470m
Tampere
Lahti
Lillehammer
St Petersburg
Bergen
Gävle
Åland
Turku
HELSINKI
Gulf of Finland
OSLO
Uppsala
Drammen
Västerås
TALLINN
Karlstad
Stavanger
STOCKHOLM
Örebro
ESTONIA
Vänern
Arendal
Norrköping
Kristiansand
Vattern
Linköping
Gotland
Gulf of Riga
Skagerrak
Göteborg
LATVIA
Jönköping
BALTIC SEA
Ålborg
RIGA
Växjö
Kattegat
DENMARK
Öland
Århus
Helsingborg
LITHUANIA
Esbjerg
COPENHAGEN
Malmö
VILNIUS
Odense
Bornholm
RUSSIA
MINSK
NORTH SEA
Kaliningrad
Hamburg
BELARUS
POLAND
GERMANY
BERLIN
WARSAW
UKRAINE

WHERE EXACTLY IS LAPLAND?

The term 'Lapland' is sometimes used to refer to the Swedish province of Lappland, or the now-defunct Finnish province of Lappi. Usually, however, Lapland is considered to span the northern parts of four countries: Norway, Sweden, Finland and the westernmost sliver of Russia's Kola Peninsula. It refers to the land traditionally inhabited by the Sámi people (page 57), who used to be called the Lapps (originally a pejorative term, this word is now little-used); the Sámi are now a minority even in their far northern homeland. The Sámi people call their traditional lands Sápmi, and you'll often see this name used instead of Lapland.

thousands of kilometres of marked trails for cross-country skiers. In the north of Finland, you can ski from November to May. **Levi** is the country's largest ski resort; it's a 15-minute drive from the airport at Kittilä, to which you can fly direct from the UK. **Ylläs** is also a haven for downhill skiers and snowboarders, as well as being home to the largest cross-country skiing network in Finland. For downhill, also try **Iso-Syöte** in southern Lapland, where authentic log cabins near the slopes provide holiday accommodation with a good chance of northern lights viewing.

THE NORTHERN LIGHTS IN FINLAND There's more to Finnish Lapland than Santa Claus. Top spots for aurora aficionados include **Lake Inari** on the Russian border where **Nellim Wilderness Hotel** (page 71) sits on the lakeshore amid the taiga forest. Its glass-roofed 'Aurora Bubble' and 'Aurora Kota' pods are specially designed for viewing the lights – they have windows facing the north sky, and beds for when the lights have gone to sleep. Its sister hotel, **Muotka Wilderness Lodge** (page 71), is located in the taiga forests of Finland's Saariselkä fells and Urho Kekkonen National Park. In the daytime, guests can take to the ski trails or dare each other to take a dip in the pool cut from the ice of the nearby river.

If ice swimming doesn't burn enough calories, try the daytime activities at the boutique **Hotel Iso-Syöte** (page 68), home to some of Finland's best slopes. Here you can clip on your downhill skis or have a go at snowshoeing, husky sledding, snowmobiling, reindeer safaris and ice fishing; Rovaniemi's Santa Claus Village and Ranua Wildlife Park are also nearby. Accommodation ranges from cottages and aurora suites with panoramic windows to the wonderful 55m^2 Eagle View Suite, which features glass walls and roof, a private sauna, and has a tree growing through the middle of it.

STEFANO ZACCARIA/S

WILDERNESS HOTELS MEDIABANK

VISIT ROVANIEMI (ROVANIEMI TOURISM)

JUHA LAINE/VISIT FINLAND

GREENLAND

How can I put this nicely? Greenland's capital, Nuuk, enjoys *average* annual temperatures of −1.6°C. And Nuuk is in the south of the country. Pack a good woolly hat, however, and Greenland is a stunning destination both for its mind-boggling beauty and its downright differentness. To start with, 80% of the country is covered in ice – Greenland's icecap covers an area more than three times the size of France. You can access one little corner of it very easily from Kangerlussuaq, home to Greenland's international airport – the edge of the icecap is just 25km away. Old Arctic hands can ski across its width. The rest of us can take an easy stroll across a tiny section (the inexperienced should go with a guide), then try out Greenland's husky sledding and musk oxen safaris.

GREENLAND AT A GLANCE

Languages Greenlandic and Danish
Population 57,000
Currency Danish krone (DKK)
Time Most of Greenland is GMT−3, with tiny pockets ranging from GMT to GMT−4
Electricity 220V; plugs have two round pins

THE NORTHERN LIGHTS IN GREENLAND Greenlandic legend relates that, when the northern lights are dancing in the sky, it means the dead are playing football with a walrus skull. Take it or leave it, Greenland's northerly location makes it an ideal spot for aurora sightings and, as its population is so sparse, it's easy to get away from the city lights. **Ilulissat** on Disko Bay is the most popular destination for tourists. This is home to the UNESCO-listed Icefjord, whose millions of sculpted icebergs, some the height of skyscrapers, glow otherworldly blue. Ilulissat's Icefjord is one of the few places where the icecap meets the sea, and its glacier is one of the most actively calving in the world. Dog sledding, skiing, snowmobiling and snowshoeing are all on offer here in the winter months. For unique accommodation try **World of Greenland** (page 71) or the more centrally located **Hotel Arctic** (page 71). You can also see the northern lights in Greenland's capital, **Nuuk**, as well as in **Kangerlussuaq**, where the international airport is located and there's easy access to the ice sheet.

A word of warning: parts of Greenland are home to healthy populations of polar bears – don't wander off into the countryside to escape light pollution without taking local advice first.

◀ **1** *Lake Inari.* **2** *One of Hotel Nangu's 'Aurora Huts'.* **3** *Santa Claus Village, Rovaniemi.* **4** *Ylläs is one of Finland's premier ski resorts.*

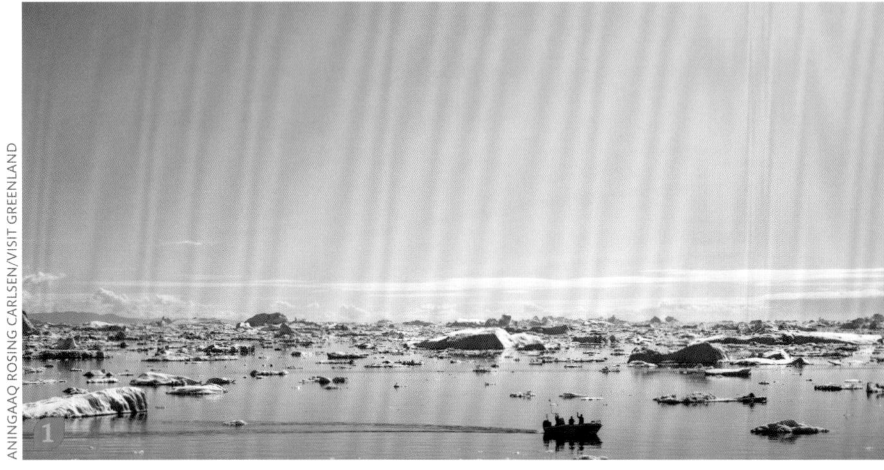
ANINGAAQ ROSING CARLSEN/VISIT GREENLAND
1

KIM RIES JENSEN/S
2

VISIT NORTH ICELAND
3

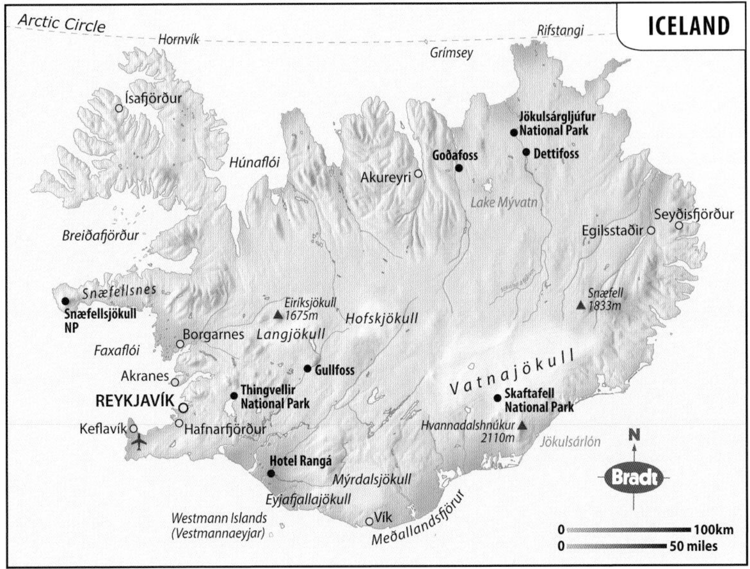

ICELAND

Iceland may not have many people – just three inhabitants to each square kilometre – but its volcanoes have a habit of drawing attention to themselves. In 2010, ash from Eyjafjallajökull caused flight disruption across Europe, while the eruption of Holuhraun in 2014–15 was the biggest Iceland had seen in 300 years. Fagradalsfjall took the limelight in 2021 with it's six-month-long lava-spewing display that followed a 6,000-year nap, As if that wasn't enough, Iceland records about 26,000 earthquakes each year – that's to say, a little more than 70 earthquakes per day.

It's certainly not the case, however, that Iceland is quaking beneath a cloud of volcanic ash. This country moulded by geothermal activity is a place of pristine beauty where geysers, volcanic peaks and lava fields create spectacular attractions. Sightseeing flights take visitors over the volcanoes, weather conditions permitting, while the more energetic can embark on a scenically mesmerising glacier

ICELAND AT A GLANCE

Language Icelandic
Population 345,000
Currency Icelandic króna (ISK)
Time GMT year-round
Electricity 220V; plugs have two round pins

◀ **1** *A boat explores the Ilulissat Icefjord.* **2** *Nuuk.* **3** *Mývatn Nature Baths.*

hike. You should always take a guided tour or hire a private guide for such walks. Indoors, boutique hotels and culinary gurus combine to create a high-end escape for those who like home comforts. Direct flights from London to Keflavík (Iceland's main international airport) take about 3 hours, making Iceland a highly accessible yet serenely exotic destination.

THE NORTHERN LIGHTS IN ICELAND The nation's capital, **Reykjavik**, is a great place for a winter getaway, with the Blue Lagoon and plenty of other attractions on its doorstep, some of them reached by Superjeep (page 59). You can sometimes see amazing northern lights displays out across the bay, even with the glow from the city. However, you don't have to travel far to escape artificial light. **Hotel Rangá** (page 72), for example, is located around a 2-hour drive from the city; here, you can enjoy aurora viewing from the comfort of a naturally heated outdoor hot tub.

NORWAY

Norway is known for its fjords and perfectly picturesque fishing villages such as those of the **Lofoten Islands**. The Lofotens, home to red-painted houses that huddle beneath soaring granite cliffs, are fabulous in winter as well as summer and temperatures are often warmer here than in other parts of Lapland. If you're looking for an authentic touch to your stay, try sleeping in a *rorbu* – a fisherman's hut on stilts. Many are now available for rent to tourists, but for an authentic experience, try to find a rickety old one rather than a shiny new imitation.

The main city in northern Norway is **Tromsø**; surrounded by mountain peaks on one side and the ocean on the other, it blends historic timber houses with a lively contemporary restaurant scene.

Stormily scenic, Europe's most northerly point is Norway's **North Cape (Nordkapp)** at 71°N, where the polar night lasts from mid-November to the end of January. You should be experienced in cold-weather driving if you're going to venture up to the cape in winter in your own vehicle, though

NORWAY AT A GLANCE

Language Norwegian (Bokm˚al and Nynorsk)
Population 5.4 million
Currency Norwegian krone (NOK)
Time GMT+1 (winter), GMT+2 (summer)
Electricity 220V; plugs have two round pins

1 The North Cape (Nordkapp) is Europe's most northerly point. 2 Tromsø. 3 The colourful houses of Longyearbyen. ▶

ANIBAL TREJO/S

MIKHAIL VARENTSOV/S

LOUIELEA/S

the last 13km is always driven in convoy following a snow plough. Don't worry if you don't have access to your own vehicle, as there's also a tourist bus from Honningsvåg.

WHERE IS FINNMARK?

Confusingly, Finnmark has absolutely nothing to do with Finland, but is the northeasternmost province of Norway. Norway's North Cape sits at Finnmark's tip.

THE NORTHERN LIGHTS IN NORWAY

The most scenic way to search out the northern lights is by sailing along Norway's coastline. Hurtigruten (page 45) offers voyages of various lengths and its ships are furnished with observation lounges. Alternatively, there are good flight connections to Tromsø, which enjoys an outstanding location for aurora viewing as it's right beneath the auroral oval. There are plenty of activities to enjoy in the city as well, including day or half-day whale-watching trips; snowmobiling and dog sledding are great activities to experience by moonlight while keeping your fingers crossed for a light show.

Svalbard, an archipelago perched high above Scandinavia at about 80°N, is part of Norway, and a winter journey to the islands constitutes a genuine adventure. Its main island is Spitsbergen; the largest settlement is Longyearbyen, which has a human population of just under 3,000 – and about the same number of polar bears. Svalbard is certainly not the easiest destination from which to see the northern lights. To start with, the sun doesn't rise between November and mid-February. While this could be a bonus – the extended hours of darkness increase your chances of seeing the lights, after all – most travellers prefer to visit from February onwards. At this time of year, you still stand a good chance of seeing the aurora yet can enjoy, for example, a multi-day snowmobiling expedition with a little bit of daylight thrown in.

SWEDEN

Northern Sweden is characterised by its tremendous expanses of pine forests and mountains. Much of this land is protected in national parks, and makes an almost limitless playground for outdoors aficionados in both summer and winter – Abisko and its surroundings are particularly recommended. Accommodation throughout Swedish Lapland, as in the rest of Scandinavia, is bright, clean and reliable. Many visitors head for at least one night to the glittering ICEHOTEL (page 77), which has helped to put the area around Kiruna firmly on the tourist map.

The northern lights over the King's Trail, Abisko ▶

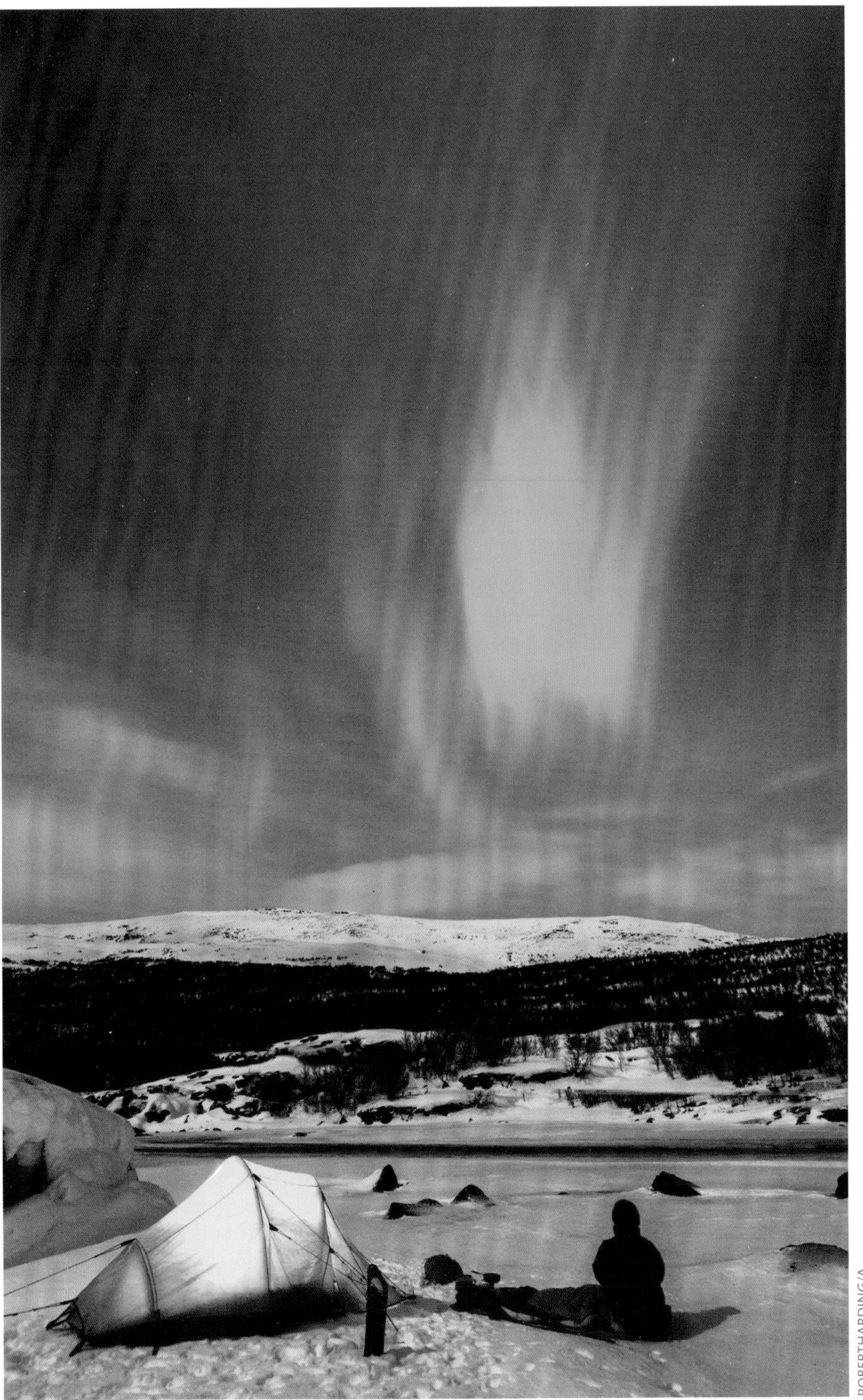

ROBERTHARDING/A

WHEN TO SEE THE NORTHERN LIGHTS

- You can only see the northern lights when the sky is dark. During the light nights of the Arctic summer, the aurora may be active – but it won't be visible because the light emitted by the aurora is much weaker than sunlight.
- You can only see the northern lights when the sky is clear of cloud. Some people claim the aurora comes out when temperatures are colder. This isn't the case – it's just that when the skies are cloudless, temperatures tend to drop.
- The northern lights are most commonly seen between 17.00 and 02.00. They don't usually exhibit for long – they may show only for a few minutes, then glide away before returning. A good display may last for no longer than a quarter or half an hour, though, if you're really lucky, it could extend to a couple of hours or longer.
- The aurora is at its most active around the equinoxes – that's to say, in March and September. The end of August and early September are good times to travel if you're a keen hiker, yet still want to try your luck with the lights – at this time of year the snow hasn't fallen, but the night-time skies are dark.
- The northern lights become more active and intense around the peak of a sunspot cycle, and in the three to four years immediately following the peak (page 14).
- The waxing and waning of the moon makes no difference to the northern lights. While a full moon lightens the sky, and may therefore reduce the visual intensity of a display, the northern lights can be seen at all stages of the moon's cycle.

POLAR NIGHTS The Arctic Circle sits at 66°33'N. At this point of latitude the Sun doesn't rise on the day of the winter solstice (and doesn't set at the summer solstice), though, as the Sun is hovering just below the horizon, the Arctic Circle never goes completely dark – there's always a bit of dusky twilight. The further north into the Arctic Circle you go, the longer the periods of winter darkness.

THE NORTHERN LIGHTS IN SWEDEN The best hub to head for in Sweden is **Kiruna**, which is a 90-minute flight from Stockholm. From there it's an easy 100km journey by road to **Abisko**, probably the best location in Europe for seeing the northern lights. Its geographical location means it enjoys a higher-than-average number of cloudless nights – thanks to the surrounding mountains that deter the rain clouds, Abisko is the driest place in Sweden. Abisko is also on the King's Trail (page 55), with its fantastic cross-country skiing opportunities.

Abisko makes the most of its clear nights with the **Aurora Sky Station**, a dedicated northern lights viewing facility that sits on top of a mountain giving huge views of the sky. The northern lights can be seen on about 50–60% of the nights that the Sky Station is open, from November to March. A chairlift takes you up to the summit where there is a café and northern lights exhibition with presentations. It is also possible to enjoy a four-course meal here. Abisko Mountain Station, at the bottom, has simple but comfortable hotel rooms as well as a hostel and self-catering options (page 77). There's a restaurant, bar, library, shop and sauna; it also rents outdoor equipment. You can combine a stay here with the nearby **ICEHOTEL** (page 77), a 1½-hour transfer away.

SWEDEN AT A GLANCE

Language Swedish
Population 10.2 million
Currency Swedish krona (SEK)
Time GMT+1 (winter), GMT+2 (summer)
Electricity 220V; plugs have two round pins

THE SOUTHERN LIGHTS

Auroral activity occurs around the magnetic South Pole just as it does around the north. However, because the southern auroral oval lies over frigid ocean and uninhabited ice pack, the southern lights, or aurora australis, are seen far less frequently than their northern counterparts (by humans at least – it's fair to assume the penguins regularly enjoy a good show). The southern lights are sometimes observed in the most southerly parts of Argentina, Chile, New Zealand and Australia, but you stand a better chance of catching a good display in the north.

3

Practical Information

WHAT TO WEAR

With the right clothing, the Arctic winter can be surprisingly comfortable. Many local suppliers will lend or rent you the thick outer garments that are expensive to buy. If your holiday consists of organised excursions such as northern lights viewing plus short dog-sledding and snowmobile trips, good-quality ski clothing should see you through. However, if you're going to be spending extended periods outdoors in sub-Arctic and Arctic weather, you should upgrade to a higher level of protection.

Apply the layer principle. It is much better to wear a number of thin layers than just a few thick ones. The air trapped in between thin layers warms to your body's temperature and acts as valuable insulation. Ensure your clothes fit well and that some of your layers are of differing sizes to avoid constriction, which will prevent air circulation and will be uncomfortable.

WHAT TO BRING

Underwear In cold conditions, it's better to wear wool, silk or synthetic polypropylene next to your skin. Avoid cotton: when you sweat, it gets cold and clammy, and doesn't dry out easily. Merino wool is excellent. On top of your base layer, you'll need to wear at least two or three additional layers, which should be made of fleece or wool. Remember that you'll need long johns as well as upper-body protection.

Outerwear A well-insulated jacket is a must, as are insulated trousers or salopettes in cold conditions. If the weather is likely to be wet you'll need waterproofs; don't take unwaterproofed down out in the rain as it soon becomes soggy and useless. Often, tour operators and hotels will loan one-piece thermal suits to put on over your jacket and trousers.

Gloves In very cold weather, it's a good idea to wear two pairs of gloves – one thick pair of mitts (mitts that don't separate the fingers keep your hands warmer) and a thin pair of gloves underneath that allow you the use of your fingers when you need to do something fiddly, yet ward off the icy

A WORD ABOUT WATER

Remember: in sub-zero temperatures, water turns to ice, so when travelling outdoors in winter, keeping your clothing dry is of the utmost importance. When walking around a boot room in just your socks, make sure you don't tread in puddles left by other people's snowy footwear. When you're outdoors, never leave your jacket with its inside facing out, or mitts with their openings facing the elements. If snow gets inside them, you'll have wet clothing. Lastly, it's always better to be a little on the cool side than to wear too much and sweat: damp clothing will make you cold.

cold for a short time, at least. If you're prone to cold extremities, you can buy carbon hand- and foot-warmers. Shake these up to activate them, pop them into your glove or boot, and they stay warm for around eight hours. If you're going to stay outdoors for an extended period, pack a spare pair of gloves – if you lose one in cold temperatures you'll soon freeze your fingers.

Footwear You'll need proper winter boots if you're going to be outside for extended periods. Many local suppliers will provide these – make sure you request a size larger than you normally wear, to comfortably accommodate extra pairs of socks. Hiking-style winter boots are suitable for simple excursions such as northern lights viewing and town-based activities, but they're not advisable for more adventurous snow-based activities as snow can easily get inside them. Make sure your footwear has good grip for walking on snow and ice.

Socks These should be made of wool, never cotton. Pack an extra pair or two in your rucksack if you're going out snowmobiling, skiing or dog sledding – if your feet become damp or wet you should change into dry socks: wet feet soon become frostbitten feet.

Hats and headwear Take a woollen or fleece hat which covers the ears, as well as a balaclava, Buff or face mask to cover mouth, nose and cheeks. Noses and cheeks are especially prone to frostbite and should be kept covered whenever possible – skin can freeze in minutes in very cold weather.

Eyewear You may need sunglasses or tinted goggles as the Sun on the snow can be dazzling. Contact-lens wearers may find the cold and dryness makes lens-wearing uncomfortable and should pack glasses as an alternative.

CHRISTINE BAGLO/VISIT NORWAY

JUHO KUVA/VISIT FINLAND

HANS-OLOF UTSI/IMAGEBANK.SWEDEN.SE

JUHO KUVA/VISIT FINLAND

Swimwear If you intend to use any sauna facilities, you may want to pack a swimsuit. There may be occasions too when you'll find yourself in an outdoor hot tub watching the northern lights overhead.

Cosmetics The northern air is very dry, and you'll need to pack plenty of lip salve. Some people have problems with water-based moisturisers – apparently the water can freeze and expand, causing burst capillaries, though I have never experienced this. Specialist products are available – ask your travel operator or local chemist.

TEMPERATURES

To give you an idea of the temperatures you'll face whilst in search of the northern lights, the average daily temperatures in degrees Celsius for Kiruna, Swedish Lapland (home of the ICEHOTEL) are: Dec –13°C / Jan –14°C / Feb –12°C / Mar –9°C / Apr –3°C. Remember, though, that the wind-chill factor can reduce these figures.

Frostbite occurs when the skin and underlying tissue freeze due to extended exposure to very low temperatures. It can affect any part of your body, but the extremities (hands, feet, ears, nose and lips) are the areas that are most likely to be affected. Nevertheless, by wearing the right clothing and taking sensible precautions frostbite can be avoided.

WINTER DRIVING

Although most short winter breaks, especially to Lapland, do not need or include car hire it is possible to hire a suitable vehicle and take off on a self-drive excursion. In Iceland, winter driving breaks are more typical. Wherever you may be, bear the following in mind:

- Take advice from a specialist travel company or local car hire firm when choosing which type of vehicle to hire. They will also have information on which areas of your chosen destination are accessible and which to avoid.
- Take local advice before setting out. If you're driving your own vehicle, make sure it is winterised. Always carry winter clothing and plenty of food as well as an emergency survival kit that includes a torch or headlamp, a shovel, sand or cat litter, and a survival candle. Mobile phone coverage may not stretch to remote areas and sometimes another vehicle will not come by for a long time. If the temperature is –30° or –40°C, if

◀ **1** *Pack a swimsuit if you plan to use any sauna or hot tub facilities.* **2** *A well-insulated jacket is a must, as are insulated trousers or salopettes.* **3** *Mitts that don't separate the fingers keep your hands warmer.* **4** *Be sure to pack some solid winter boots.*

HEMIS/A

you have an accident and you can't keep your vehicle's engine running, and if you're not carrying proper winter clothing, you'll freeze fast.

- Drive slowly and according to the local road conditions. By law, car rental companies across the region are required to fit winter tyres for improved grip. Some, but not all, will be studded. You'll soon know which you have once you pull away – the studded variety make a faint tick, tick, tick sound on tarmac. Car hire companies also offer a support system in case of breakdowns.
- Keep the tank as full as possible and always refuel when you have the opportunity.
- If you do have an accident or breakdown and need to keep the engine running to keep warm, make sure the exhaust pipe is not blocked with snow and always keep a window open to let in fresh air, otherwise there is the danger of accidental asphyxiation. You may prefer to burn a survival candle than to keep the vehicle's engine running.
- Lastly, if you pass a broken-down vehicle, you *must* stop. Your failure to help could be critical.

NORTHERN LIGHTS FORECASTING

There are three different time scales that are used for northern lights forecasting: 30–90 minutes (OVATION), three days and 27 days. Many websites feature all three of these forecasting tools, including NOAA Space Weather Prediction Center (w swpc.noaa.gov/products/aurora-30-minute-forecast) and The Geophysical Institute at the University of Alaska (w gi.alaska.edu/auroraforecast). You can view predicted activity in all auroral regions and sign up for email alerts that tell you when activity rises above a certain level.

OVATION FORECAST For a short-term forecast, the OVATION model is used. It tells us what we're going to see in the next 30–90 minutes by measuring solar wind speed and the interplanetary magnetic field, 1.6 million kilometres up from Earth. This is a great tool if you're already in situ, but don't want to spend all night sitting outside in the cold.

THREE-DAY FORECAST The three-day northern lights forecast is generally accurate – it's much more reliable than the weather forecast. The forecast corresponds to the planetary magnetic index (Kp) on a scale of one to nine, with one being very low activity and nine a humdinging dazzler.

◀ *A hardy vehicle such as a Superjeep is crucial for off-road excursions in extreme conditions.*

A tripod is a must for photographing the northern lights

PAUL ZIZKA/VISIT GREENLAND

27-DAY FORECAST It takes 27 days for the Sun to make a complete rotation on its axis. This forecast works on the basis that the solar phenomena that create the northern lights – sunspots and so on – return to face Earth every 27 days, and so auroral activity is likely to be similar at 27-day intervals while those phenomena persist.

HOW TO PHOTOGRAPH THE NORTHERN LIGHTS

Most of the professional northern lights photos you see will have been taken with a DSLR camera. However, it is absolutely possible to take great aurora pics with your phone if you use the manual settings or download a specialist app (see opposite). It is worth noting that, unless you have a fisheye lens, your camera will capture only a fragment of the sky, and during a really spectacular display, the northern lights work their magic across 360°. It's easy to get carried away with photography – but for the best experience, remember to take a few moments just to step back and enjoy the show.

DSLR PHOTOGRAPHY For the best results you'll want a lens with a wide aperture (f2.8 is good enough, f2.4 is better and f1.4 is best) and a wide angle. For fast-moving displays, an exposure of 5 to 10 seconds should do the trick, and you'll need to crank the ISO up to 800 or more. Experiment to see what is sufficient in terms of ISO – you don't want to go higher than you need to as you risk noise in your photo. If the lights are doing more of a slow dance, go for a longer exposure of 10 to 20 seconds, and a lower ISO of 400–800. If it's just a green glow, you can luxuriate in a 30-second exposure and soak in all that extra light.

Given the long exposure, a tripod is a must. Experienced northern lights photographers often wrap foam around their tripod's legs to prevent themselves from touching the metal with bare fingers (the skin sticks). Many photographers prefer to use a cable release – but just pressing the button can also work well. It's also a good idea to wear a pair of thin gloves to protect your skin from frostbite – but remember the protection thin gloves offer will last only a few minutes in cold conditions. Carry thick mitts, too. Plus, you'll need to take a headlamp so you can see what you're doing in the dark.

Camera batteries die fast in cold temperatures. Always carry a spare, and keep it tucked into your clothing, close to your skin to keep it warm. Even better, buy a battery grip and load it with lithium AA batteries – these keep their charge for a reasonable period. Try not to take your camera indoors with you as the lens will fog up with the change in temperature and, when you go outside again, the condensation will turn to ice. If you must take your camera indoors, put it in a plastic bag – ziplock seals work well. Make sure you take a micro-fibre cloth to wipe fog and ice from your lens.

When selecting a location for your photography, try to find a place with some foreground – a tent or building lit from the inside, or some trees – that will give your pictures perspective. Shoot in RAW if you can, to give you greater scope for manipulation later. Use the manual focus, and set the focus to infinity, then open up the aperture as wide as your lens will allow. If you can, turn off the LCD display as its light will interfere with your vision through the viewfinder in the dark. Then just point and shoot and pray.

TAKING PHOTOS WITH YOUR PHONE Can you shoot good photos of the aurora with a smartphone? Absolutely you can – and some features, such as iPhone's live photos, work very well for the northern lights.

Check out your phone's camera settings. If it allows you to change the ISO, shutter speed and exposure, follow the advice for DSLR cameras above. Alternatively, download an app such as Apple's Northern Lights Photo Taker. If you can't alter your phone's settings, you can download a slow shutter speed app such as Slow Shutter Cam, LongExpo or NightCap. You must use some kind of tripod, even when using a phone, but it doesn't need to be expensive. A cheap smartphone stand will do the job – just remember that it will break more easily in cold temperatures.

MAKING MOVIES It is virtually impossible to film the northern lights using a regular movie recorder. To record moving images of the northern lights, expensive specialist equipment is required.

TOUR OPERATORS

UK

Best Served Scandinavia 020 7838 5956; e enquire@best-served.co.uk; w best-served.co.uk. As an out & out tailor-made Scandinavia specialist, Best Served Scandinavia is a go-to tour operator for holidays to the Nordic regions, with trips to Finland, Greenland, Iceland, Norway, Sweden & Canada.

Discover the World 01737 218800; e travel@discover-the-world.co.uk; w discover-the-world.com. As a leading specialist in tailor-made travel for more than 3 decades, Discover the World offers a wide variety of northern lights holidays to Sweden, Finland, Norway, Iceland, Canada & Alaska, with a full range of winter activities. Fly direct between London & Kiruna to reach the ICEHOTEL at Jukkasjärvi in just 3½hrs.

Hurtigruten 020 3582 8772; e uk.sales@hurtigruten.com; w hurtigruten.co.uk/destinations/norway. Hurtigruten's various northern lights cruises are based around Norway's fjords & Arctic coastline. In addition to mainstream itineraries, it offers specialist trips such as astronomy voyages.

Kirker Holidays 020 7593 2283; e travel@kirkerholidays.com; w kirkerholidays.com. Since 1986, Kirker Holidays has provided carefully crafted tailor-made holidays to a range of

WHY ARE MY PHOTOS SO GREEN?

The first time I photographed the northern lights, I was still using a film camera. On my return home, I took my film to be developed. 'These are amazing,' said the man in the shop when I collected my prints. 'Are the northern lights really that green?' I looked at my pictures and had to say, well, actually, no.

In those photos, the aurora came out a dazzling emerald – whereas, with my naked eye, I had seen more of a milky green. This is a common theme with northern lights photos. Given the long exposure time, the camera picks up more than our eyes are able to see. Colours become more saturated. The camera sometimes picks up other hues – usually red – that you hadn't noticed at the time. This is because the human eye sees the colour green more easily. On occasion, the camera is even able to photograph an aurora that the eye didn't even know was there.

JORMA LUHTA/VISIT FINLAND

destinations throughout Europe & beyond, including some of the best locations for viewing the northern lights in Iceland, Sweden & Norway. Kirker's team of experts has first-hand experience of every hotel & will help you to plan the perfect itinerary including flights from your local airport, carefully selected accommodation & excursions with local expert guides.

Nordic Experience 01206 708888; e reservations@nordicexperience.co.uk; w nordicexperience.co.uk. Nordic Experience is a leading independent UK tour operator specialising in tailor-made holidays & private tours to Finland, Sweden, Norway, Iceland & Greenland, as well as exclusive small-group Father Christmas & New Year adventures. It draws on the expert knowledge of its staff, all of whom have travelled extensively in the region. They are on hand to offer you first-class recommendations as to when & where to travel, & how to maximise your chances of viewing the aurora borealis.

Regent Holidays 020 3588 2971; e regent@regentholidays.co.uk; w regent-holidays.co.uk. With over 40 years' experience, Regent Holidays offers an extensive range of northern lights holidays to Iceland, Greenland, Finland, Norway & Sweden, including group tours, city breaks & fly-drives. In addition to its suggested itineraries, the Bristol-based team of knowledgeable & experienced travel specialists can tailor-make your perfect winter itinerary to incorporate a variety of activities including husky & reindeer sledding, snowmobiling, Arctic cruises, snowshoeing & more.

Sunvil 020 8758 4722; e discovery@sunvil.co.uk; w sunvil.co.uk. Sunvil uses its local knowledge & first-hand experience to carefully-craft holidays in Swedish Lapland & northern Norway to meet individual requirements. Tours range from Arctic Svalbard to the wilderness of Finnmark, the university city of Tromsø, the aurora hot spot of Abisko, the ICEHOTEL in Jukkasjärvi & more.

CANADA

The Great Canadian Travel Group 204 949 0199, 1 800 661 3830; e sales@gctravel.ca; w greatcanadiantravel.com. The Great Canadian Travel Company has been operating tours to the top (& bottom) of the world since 1980, specialising in Arctic Canada, Greenland, Iceland, Faroe Islands, Norway & Antarctica. Experiences include northern lights viewing, wildlife safaris, escorted tours, expedition cruises & independent self-drive programmes. It caters to both independent travellers & small groups, offering personalised individual itineraries & customised group services.

Northern Tales 1 867 667 6054; e info@northerntales.ca; w northerntales.ca. This is your one-stop shop for northern lights & winter adventure in Yukon, with an award-winning aurora tour. It also offers dog mushing, snowmobiling, ice fishing, cabin rentals, trips to the Arctic Circle & ice roads.

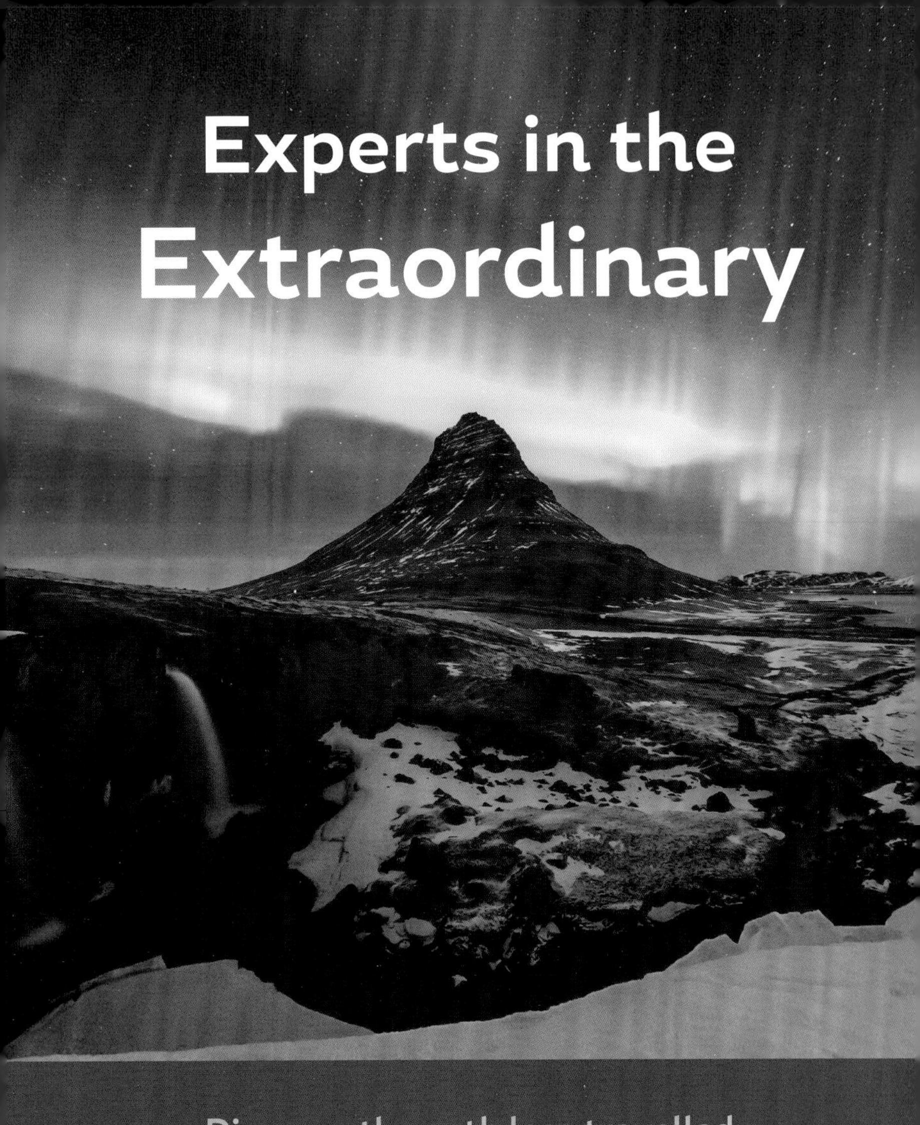
Experts in the
Extraordinary

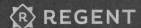

4

Beyond the Northern Lights

But what will you do in the daytime? The northern lights are visible only during the hours of darkness, and are best seen in rural locations away from the bright lights of inhabited areas. Some visitors will happily while away the day reading a book, but for the rest, entrepreneurial northerners have created a whole winter wonderland of diversions.

SOMETHING FOR THE DAYTIME

DOG SLEDDING Dog-sledding trips are a bit like pieces of string: you can cut them as long or as short as you like. Many operators offer outings of an hour or two, where you'll sit in the sledge and an experienced musher will drive you through snow-laden forests and across frozen lakes, on the lookout for Arctic foxes, ptarmigan or even elk if you're lucky. Some excursions let you buddy up and take it in turns to mush. The more adventurous, however, might like to opt for a longer, hands-on experience. On such specialist tours, you'll mush your own team across various trails and terrain and really get to know your dogs, looking after them over a period of three to four days or more. The longer you can spend with your dogs, the more you'll gain from the experience.

SNOWMOBILING Snowmobiles, or skidoos, are a bit like jet skis on snow. They provide a useful way of travelling efficiently across frozen landscapes and they allow visitors to see much more of their surroundings than they would if they stick to the road network.

Trips can last anything from an hour to a day or even longer, and in many locations special evening snowmobile trips take you in search of the aurora. For those who are afraid of the cold, they are warmer by far than a dog sled (they often have heated handlebars, and the engine helps keep you toasty). You will need a full driving licence to drive a snowmobile.

CROSS-COUNTRY SKIING If you want to combine your northern lights viewing with the thrill of cross-country skiing on trails in the daytime, the two destinations are Abisko in Sweden, and Levi, Saariselkä and Ylläs in Finland.

Dog sledding in Finland

WILDERNESS HOTELS MEDIABANK

BÅRD BASBERG/LOEN SKYLIFT/VISIT NORWAY

HENRIK TRYGG/IMAGEBANK.SWEDEN.SE

VISIT NORTH ICELAND

MATT HAGE/TRAVEL ALASKA

Abisko sits at the beginning of the legendary King's Trail, or Kungsleden as it is known in Swedish, which runs for 440km southwards to Hemavan. The trail passes through the pristine wilderness of four national parks and a nature reserve. Most people take a few weeks to ski the whole shebang but you can just do a section – the most popular is the first 86km between Abisko and Kebnekaise. Accommodation is in cabins dotted along the way; various tour operators offer supported trips for those who'd prefer not to go it alone.

There are 330km of maintained cross-country trails in Finland's Ylläs; 38km are illuminated during the dark months. Many of the trails fall within the Pallas-Ylläs National Park. Cafés sit along many of the routes, and lessons are available in both Äkäslompolo and Ylläsjärvi, the villages that serve the area. Elsewhere, Levi has 230km of cross-country tracks, as well as excellent downhill skiing, and the main trails are lit from 06.00 until 23.00, with cafés along the way. Saariselkä is another good bet, with 200km of tracks.

Cross-country skiing is a way of life for the locals in Alaska and northern Canada where frozen lakes and rivers, and summer hiking trails, all make great ski routes once the snow falls. All the major destinations covered by this book have cross-country ski clubs that can advise on trails and conditions.

ALPINE SKIING Scandinavian ski resorts tend to be smaller and less developed than those of the Alps but the great advantages are that the snow is reliable, the pistes are uncrowded, and you can combine your downhill endeavours with northern lights viewing, dog sledding and even a visit to Santa.

Levi is Finland's largest resort with 43 pistes and rapidly developing lift system. Another good option for downhill skiing is the **Ylläs** area of Finland, which has 62 slopes and 30 lifts. It's excellent for off-piste, telemark and cross-country skiing, too. **Iso-Syöte** and **Ruka** also come recommended.

Björkliden in Sweden has 23 runs and good off-piste opportunities. It's conveniently close to Abisko National Park from where you can take a chairlift up to the Aurora Sky Station (page 35) for northern lights viewing and the ICEHOTEL (page 77) in Jukkasjärvi. You can either stay in Björkliden and drive over to Abisko in the evenings, or stay at the

◀ **1** *Snowshoeing in Norway.* **2** *Björkliden in Sweden has good off-piste skiing opportunities.* **3** *Horseriding excursions are popular in Iceland.* **4** *Snowmobiles are a fun and useful mode of transport in Alaska.*

Sámi woman cooking inside a lavvu

THE SÁMI

- The Sámi's traditional lands span the northern parts of Norway, Sweden, Finland and Russia's Kola Peninsula but, even in these areas, the Sámi are now a minority. The Sámi refer to their land as Sápmi.
- The Sámi were once called the Lapps, which means 'scraps of cloth' in Scandinavian languages. Many Sámi people consider the term to be derogatory.
- Sámi language and culture declined in the first half of the 20th century, especially in Norway where the Sámi population is greatest, due to assimilation and cultural suppression.
- In recent decades, Sámi language and culture have been promoted. There are separate Sámi parliaments in Norway, Sweden and Finland (Russia does not recognise the Sámi as an ethnic minority group), and in these countries the Sámi people share responsibility for the management of their territorial lands.
- There are estimated to be 80,000–100,000 Sámi people living in Scandinavia and western Russia today. About half live in Norway; Sweden has the next largest population.
- In appearance, Sámi look very similar to other Scandinavian people. They are often blond-haired and blue-eyed.
- There are many different Sámi languages. Although the languages are linked – they're related to Finnish and Estonian – not all Sámi can understand each other. Not all Sámi people can speak a Sámi language, but all can speak the language of the country where they live. A few schools across northern Scandinavia teach most classes in the Sámi language.
- Traditional Sámi industries include reindeer husbandry, hunting and fishing – but only 10% of Sámi herd reindeer today. Modern-day reindeer herding uses snowmobiles, helicopters, mobile phones and lorries to transport the stock.
- The Sámi flag is vibrantly coloured, with a half-blue, half-red circle over a background of red, yellow, green and blue panels and stripes. It was raised for the first time in August 1986.
- Traditional Sámi dress varies between regions, but often consists of bright blue wool or felt tunics with red and yellow embroidery and bands for men, and dresses for women in a similar style. Both men and women wear reindeer-skin boots.

Abisko Mountain Station and ski down into the Björkliden trail system from the top of Abisko's chairlift. Also nearby are the downhill resorts of Riksgränsen and Narvik, while the area between Abisko and Narvik offers fantastic ski touring possibilities. Mount Nuolja is recommended for off-piste enthusiasts.

Alaska's most popular resort is Alyeska, near Anchorage, where lifts open late at the weekend, offering the chance to ski beneath the aurora. Alaska is also known for its extensive heli-skiing and cat-skiing opportunities.

SNOWSHOEING Snowshoes have long been worn by residents of the north to allow them to walk on deep snow without sinking. Flat, outsized plates strapped to your boots, they spread your weight over a wider area, keeping you above rather than in the snow. The snowshoes of bygone days looked like giant tennis rackets, but now they come in all colours and materials. A tourist snowshoeing excursion will generally involve going for a hike with a guide who will point out animal tracks, local points of interest and share stories of the area.

HORSERIDING The Icelanders are proud of their horses and are determined to keep the breeding of Icelandic horses pure. Since AD982, laws have forbidden horses of any other breed from being imported into the country and an Icelandic horse, once exported, may not return. Visually distinctive, the horses possess two unique gaits as a natural addition to the standard walk, trot and canter. Visitors to Iceland can take horseriding excursions throughout the year. During the winter months, they'll be provided with insulated clothing. Visitors to the ICEHOTEL in Sweden can also ride an Icelandic horse to see moose and, hopefully, the aurora. These horses are suitable for novices and children over the age of 12.

VOLCANOES The mid-Atlantic ridge cuts neatly through the middle of Iceland. This is where the Eurasian and North American tectonic plates are pulling apart at a rate of just over 2cm a year, giving rise to the geothermal liveliness for which the country is famous. One of the most popular volcanoes for visitors to Iceland is **Fagradalsfjall**, whose eruption in 2021 lasted for six months. It's about an hour's drive from Reykjavik and 30 minutes from Keflavík airport. There are many short hiking routes to see the crater and newly formed lava. The more energetic can also climb the famously disruptive and hard-to-pronounce **Eyjafjallajökull**, whose ash stopped air traffic in Europe for several days in 2010. It's a strenuous hike of 8–10 hours, and spectacularly beautiful. If that sounds a bit much, Eyjafjallajökull can also be visited by Superjeep, and some Superjeep tours include northern lights hunting on the volcano's glacier. Sightseeing flights over many of Iceland's volcanoes take to the skies regularly, weather permitting.

VISITING SANTA CLAUS The Americans may claim that Santa comes from the town of North Pole, Alaska (named in the 1950s by a development company that hoped to attract a toy factory to its rather chilly real estate), and the Russians may insist that he's theirs but, deep down, everyone knows that Santa lives in Lapland. Of all the Scandinavian nations, it's the Finns who trade most enthusiastically on the Christmas connection. Following a myth engendered by the Finnish Broadcasting Corporation in the early decades of the 20th century, Finns will tell you that Father Christmas comes from Korvatunturi, a mountain in Urho Kekkonen National Park. But Korvatunturi is impractical for money-making folk – it's just too remote – so the city of **Rovaniemi** cashed in on its relative geographical proximity and declared itself the 'official hometown of Santa Claus'. Now there's a Santa Claus Village, including Santa's main post office, a 'Santapark' theme park, a bunch of elves and a sled-load of reindeer, as well as a science centre and cultural attractions relating to Lapland's nature, art and history.

SAUNAS, SPAS AND HOT SPRINGS The Finns just can't help themselves – there's nothing they like more, it seems, than to take off their clothes, get very sweaty, and then go for a roll in the snow. The good news is, tourists can indulge in the experience, too (for many, it's a highlight of their trip). Almost all accommodation comes complete with a **sauna** and some rooms have their own private hot tub too. In Alaska, **Chena Hot Springs** (w chenahotsprings.com) are open daily until just before midnight; there is also an ice museum, dog sledding and aurora tours. **Eclipse Nordic Hot Springs** (w eclipsenordichotsprings.ca) in Whitehorse is open 10.00–23.00, or for private rentals both during the day and after public hours. For those concerned with their coiffure, there's even an annual hair-freezing contest.

Given its propensity for geothermal hubble bubble, it's not surprising that Iceland is choc-a-bloc with hot springs and spas. Sculpted by volcanic eruptions across the ages, the Mývatn area of Iceland has a striking beauty defined by craters and lava columns, sulphurous steam vents and hot pools that bubble and burp. Visitors can bathe in the **Mývatn Nature Baths** (w myvatnnaturebaths.is), whose milky-blue lagoon keeps a year-round temperature of 38–40°C. The **Blue Lagoon** (w bluelagoon.com), with its steamy pastel-blue pool set amid a jet-black lavascape, is one of Iceland's

Fagradalsfjall erupting, Iceland.

DANIEL FREYR/S

REINDEER SLEDDING

My reindeer was called Girjebahta, which means 'Spotty Bottom' in the Sámi language. She was a beautiful creature with pale fur, long, elegantly arching antlers – and an attitude that, had Santa been foolish enough to select her, would have put the kybosh on Christmas.

I was with a group of fellow reindeer novices in Swedish Lapland. Our Sámi guide, Nils-Erik, had shown us how to lasso the reindeer's antlers with bright orange rubber rope. Then he'd harnessed one creature to each sled, instructed us to kneel one person to each, and to make a circuit of the track that ran between the snow-laden spruce trees. But I'd only covered a few metres before Spotty ran out of steam and, rather than running, pretended to nibble at a sparse little twig that lay on the path before her.

'Woop woop,' I shouted (*woop woop* is Sámi for 'get a move on') and I whacked her on the bottom with the rope. Spotty turned and pouted, and planted her pretty little hooves in the snow. But then a sprightlier reindeer appeared from behind and Spotty's competitive spirit was spurred.

Neck and neck, the two animals galloped. Our wooden sleds leapt from the peaks of ruts in the snow, and clattered into its divots. Antlers almost clashed, sleds seemed certain to derail, and as the opposing team tried to squeeze by on the inside I had to duck low to avoid a disembowelment. Then, just when disaster seemed inevitable, Spotty stopped stock still and refused to move once more.

'You have to show the reindeer who's boss,' Nils-Erik explained wearily, having trudged out around the track to lead us in. I quietly suspected that both my reindeer and I knew which of us that was.

Later, we sat in a *lavvu* – the large, conical Sámi tent – and ate reindeer meat that Nils-Erik had fried in a gargantuan pan over a fire, followed by stewed loganberries. There are around 200,000 reindeer in Sweden, Nils-Erik told us, and almost all of them are domesticated by the country's 20,000-strong Sámi population. Their antlers grow in summer – as much as a centimetre each day – and then drop off in autumn and winter.

most iconic tourist attractions. Water temperatures remain at 37–39°C year-round, and spa treatments and massages are available. In West Iceland, also check out the **Húsafell Canyon Baths** (w husafell.com/activities/husafell-canyon-baths) and **Krauma Baths** (w krauma.is). **Geosea** (w geosea.is) clings to a cliffside on the northern coast, while **Secret Lagoon** (w secretlagoon.is), a 90-minute drive east of Reykjavik, claims it is Iceland's oldest swimming pool – locals have been bathing here since the 19th century.

Nils-Erik had spent the previous four days herding reindeer. He and his companions had separated the animals into the smaller groups that belong to each family – his parents owned a thousand or so of them. It's hard physical work; Nils-Erik revealed that he went to the gym to toughen up for the reindeer-herding season. But the Sámi people nowadays use snowmobiles to travel and, where feasible, they even truck their reindeer by road. As for the *lavvu*, nobody sleeps in one anymore – which was just as well for Nils-Erik.'I'm allergic to the reindeer skins that cover the ground,' he told us, 'and the smoke from the fire sets off my asthma.'

WILDERNESS HOTELS MEDIABANK

Reindeer sledding with Wilderness Hotels.

WINTER WEDDINGS White stilettos might be out of the question; and brides, don't forget your faux-fur stole. But dress properly for the occasion and an ice chapel venue can take your wedding to a whole new shade of dazzling white. The **ICEHOTEL** in Sweden (page 77) has a winter Ice Ceremony Hall that is open from December to April, newly designed each year, and in the spring returns to the river. Also built afresh each winter is the **Kemi SnowCastle** (page 69) in Finnish Lapland, constructed with snow and ice

TRAVEL MANITOBA

VISIT NORTH ICELAND

GOVERNMENT OF YUKON

from the Gulf of Bothnia. You can tie the knot in its SnowChapel and – who knows? – maybe the aurora will take the first dance.

POLAR BEARS Probably the most accessible place to see polar bears in the wild is **Churchill**, Manitoba, which calls itself the 'polar bear capital of the world'. Nearly 1,000 bears gather here in October and November as they wait for Hudson Bay to freeze so that they can hunt the seals that live beneath its ice. Visitors can travel out to see polar bears in specially designed 'tundra buggies'. Sometimes you can even take a trip to the polar bear jail where those that have strayed too far into town serve their time before being released back into the wild, but you can only visit when the jail has no inmates.

DOG-SLED RACES Two of the mushing world's most famous races take place in Alaska and Yukon during the winter months. In February, the **Yukon Quest** (w yukonquest.com) has 450-, 250- and 100-mile trails between Whitehorse and Dawson City. Pre-Covid, this was a 1,000-mile race between Whitehorse and Fairbank. However, musher numbers dwindled, and in 2022 the partnership between the Alaskan and Yukon organisers of the race was dissolved. In March the **Iditarod** (w iditarod.com) covers the full 1,000 miles between Anchorage and the coastal village of Nome. The Iditarod celebrates the serum run of 1925: when diphtheria broke out in Nome, doctors feared an epidemic. The only way to save the village was to transport serum by dog-sled relay, day and night over 700 miles of frozen wilderness. (Gay and Laney Salisbury's telling of the story in their brilliant book *The Cruellest Miles* is a must-read for anyone interested in Alaska and its history; page 93). Visitors can spectate from the start and finish, and various points along the routes of both races including the wonderfully comfortable Winterlake Lodge (page 66).

Europe's longest dog-sled race is the 1,000km **Finnmarksløpet** (w finnmarkslopet.no), which runs across Norway's Finnmark region each March.

GOLD-RUSH HISTORY Alaska and northern Canada are rich with gold-rush history – many of the towns owe their very existence to the gold rushes and the infrastructure that sprung up to house and feed the stampeders. The big one was the **Klondike**, in Canada's Yukon, to which an estimated 100,000

◀**1** *Churchill, Manitoba calls itself the 'polar bear capital of the world'.* **2** *Geosea is one of Iceland's many hot springs.* **3** *The Yukon Quest dog-sled race takes place between Whitehorse and Dawson City.*

hopefuls swarmed in 1898. Visitors to Whitehorse can find out more at the **MacBride Museum** or, better still, add a few days to their trip by taking in **Dawson City**, the town that was created by the Klondike Gold Rush and whose historic charm remains almost unspoilt.

WHERE TO STAY

From ice hotels to igloos to secluded log cabins with roaring wood stoves, when in search of the lights you'll have a variety of accommodation options. Here are a few of the more interesting.

ALASKA

Alyeska Resort (w alyeskaresort.com) Alyeska is essentially a ski resort, but it has northern lights too. It's convenient, by Alaska's standards at any rate – just under an hour's drive from Anchorage – and there's a northern lights wake-up service.

Iniakuk Lake Wilderness Lodge (w gofarnorth.com) Far from the beaten track yet supremely comfortable, Iniakuk bills itself as 'luxury in the far north'. Located in the Brooks Range, 100km north of the Arctic Circle, it's accessible only by ski plane in winter or float plane in summer. It offers dog-sledding expeditions and tuition in aurora photography.

Winterlake Lodge (w withinthewild.com/lodges/winterlake-lodge) Truly remote, yet properly luxurious, Winterlake Lodge is one of the world's magical spots – accessible only by ski plane in winter (open from February) and float plane in summer. Owners Carl and Kirsten Dixon keep sled dogs and offer mushing trips that take in the famous Iditarod trail, on which the lodge sits (page 65). Cross-country skiing, snowshoeing and winter camping are also available, as are fat biking, glacier treks and helicopter tours, while indoors there are yoga sessions, massages and daily cooking classes – and Kirsten's cooking is legendary. Come nightfall, the hot tub on the terrace makes an ideal spot for lying back and watching the northern lights.

CANADA

Blachford Lake Lodge (w blachfordlakelodge.com) Like Winterlake and Iniakuk Lake in Alaska, Blachford Lodge, near Yellowknife in Northwest Territories, is accessible only by ski or float plane. Activities include

1 *Kayaking on Finger Lake at Winterlake Lodge, Alaska.*
2 *Igloo building at Blachford Lake Lodge, Canada.* ▶

1

WITHIN THE WILD

2

MARTINA GEBAROVSKA + BLACHFORD LAKE LODGE

snowmobiling, skiing, snowshoeing, igloo building, winter camping, ice fishing and skating – or, for something more relaxing, you can watch the aurora from the hot tub, solar flares permitting.

Inn on the Lake (w innonthelake.ca) Another very comfortable lodge, Inn on the Lake sits on the shores of Marsh Lake, just outside Whitehorse in the Yukon Territory. Fine dining round the lodge family table is a feature here, with a focus on local ingredients. Dog sledding, ice fishing, show shoeing, snowmobiling, scenic flights and the rest are available in the daytime.

FINLAND

Arctic Treehouse Hotel (w arctictreehousehotel.com) Sitting just outside Rovaniemi in Finnish Lapland, this beautiful contemporary hotel combines Lappish traditions with modern Scandi design. It's won a plethora of awards for architecture, design, cuisine and comfort. Choose between TreeHouse Suites, Arctic GlassHouses with private sauna, woodburner and terrace or, at the top end, the ArcticScene Executive Suites, which sit in glorious solitude in the snowy forest. The hotel provides fat bikes, kicksleds, toboggans and snowshoes free of charge. You can also sign up for husky, reindeer and snowmobile safaris, and a whole smorgasbord of winter activities. Floor-to-ceiling glass windows give panoramic views of the aurora when she's out – and of the forest the rest of the time. And it's within walking distance of the Santa Claus Village.

Hotel Iso-Syöte (w hotelli-isosyote.fi) This is a mountaintop retreat with an emphasis on panoramic views of the sky, so it's a top spot for viewing the aurora with a dash of luxury. Most extravagant is the Eagle Suite, whose walls and roof are made from glass so you can just lie back in bed and watch the northern lights at play. There's also a private sauna and a tree growing through the middle of the room. Aurora suites, as the name suggests, also have a focus on sky views, or if that all sounds too comfortable, you can spend the night in a snow igloo instead. Daytime activities include cross-country and downhill skiing (page 55), husky and reindeer safaris, snowshoeing and snowmobiling.

Kakslauttanen Arctic Resort (w kakslauttanen.fi) If it's a personal igloo you're after, look no further than Kakslauttanen Arctic Resort. You can choose between an ice-cold snow igloo, where the temperature hovers around –5°C or, if that's a little on the chilly side, try one of the glass-roofed igloos, which are perfect for watching the northern lights from bed. Recent additions to the resort include the *kelo*-glass igloos, which combine the glass roof of the bedroom with a cosy cabin built from Lapland's *kelo* pine. Log chalets are also available for up to ten people as well as riverside chalets, and the Traditional House that survived the battle at Mäntyvaara, which was part of the Soviet Union's invasion of Finland in 1939. The resort has three riverside smoke saunas that can hold up to 100 sweaty bodies at once – in cold weather, they'll cut a hole in the river ice so you can take a dip afterwards.

Luxury Lodge L7 (w luxurylodge.fi) Lodge L7 sits on the edge of the Pallas-Ylläs National Park, 6km away from the ski resort of Ylläs, and is surrounded by 28ha of private forest. You can snowshoe or cross-country ski direct from the hotel to the ski resort. The lodge also has its own guides who will take you on snowmobile, husky and reindeer safaris. There's a big communal living room with fireplace, an outdoor jacuzzi and a restaurant as well as a ski waxing room. Luxury Lodge also owns the smaller **Ylläs Humina** hotel (w yllashumina.com), on the shores of Lake Äkäslompolo, which has fine dining and a pub, saunas and skiing.

Northern Lights Village (w northernlightsvillage.com) These are actually two separate villages: Levi and Saariselkä. Both offer high-end accommodation in glass-roofed cabins specifically designed for watching the northern lights. The Levi village also has larger aurora suites that sleep up to five people and have a private sauna. Aurora hunting, snowmobiling, huskies, reindeer, visits to Santa Claus Village, snow sports and cultural outings that invite you to explore Sámi culture are all on offer. Both areas are excellent for cross-country skiing, while Levi is home to Finland's largest alpine ski resort (page 55).

SnowCastle (w experience365.fi) Think Disney in the deep freeze. The SnowCastle in Kemi has a fairy-tale theme with turrets and crenellations, and sculptures of rugged heroes and floating princesses carved into the snow walls. There are two parts to the SnowCastle: the snowy fortress that is built anew each year for the winter season, and SnowExperience 365 which is open year-round. Within the SnowCastle you can stay in the sub-zero rooms of the SnowHotel (temperature around –5°C), or opt for a glass villa on the shore of Bothnia Bay where floor-to-ceiling windows give great views both day and night. A unique activity here is a day cruise on the icebreaker ship, *Sampo*, which voyages through the frozen Gulf of Bothnia; passengers are invited to dress in survival suits and indulge in a little 'ice floating' themselves. Or, for a different kind of once-in-a-lifetime experience, you can get married in the SnowChapel (page 63).

1

ARCTIC TREEHOUSE HOTEL | ROVANIEMI, FINLAND

ARCTIC BOUTIQUE HOTEL ISO SYÖTE & SAFARIS

STAR ARCTIC HOTEL

TIMO LAAPOTTI/KEMI TOURISM LTD

Star Arctic Hotel (w stararctichotel.com) This mountaintop retreat sits 225km above the Arctic Circle, on top of the Kaunispää fell, with views over Saariselkä. Aurora glass cabins and scenic view suites are available, as well as full packages including husky rides, reindeer safaris, fat-bike rental, snowmobiling and, of course, aurora hunting.

Wilderness Hotels (w wildernesshotels.fi) Wilderness Hotels owns four sister resorts in northern Lapland: Nellim, Nangu, Inari and Muotka, all located near Ivalo, about 350km north of the Arctic Circle. Each offers a variety of accommodation from rooms in the main lodge and log cabins to aurora huts, some of which have glass roofs angled towards the northern sky. Daytime activities include husky safaris, snowmobiling, ice fishing, showshoeing, cross-country skiing and aurora viewing once the sky is dark. There is some variety between hotels depending on the location; at Muotka, for example, you can cross-country ski on the trails in the Urho Kekkonen National Park, while at Inari you can enjoy a 'cultural day' in the nearby Sámi village or visit the local reindeer farm. All four hotels have restaurants specialising in the local Lappish cuisine and regional ingredients – think moose stew, Arctic char, reindeer, and so on.

GREENLAND

Hotel Arctic (w hotelarctic.com) Situated in Ilulissat, right on the shores of the UNESCO-listed Icefjord, this is the world's northernmost four-star hotel. It's not a boutique design hotel in the way that many of the others in this section are, but you'll get your trip-of-a-lifetime experience with the famous icebergs of the Icefjord floating right outside your window. The Icefjord Centre tells visitors about the area's history and the impact of climate change; you can also take a dog-sledding trip or scenic flight, and go ice fishing, show shoeing or northern lights hunting. Ilulissat itself is big by Greenland's standards – 4,500 inhabitants – and the locals live a traditional life often using dog sleds for transport and making handicrafts from sealskin. There are various other accommodation options overlooking the icebergs as well such as the Hotel Icefjord – check out Visit Greenland's website (w visitgreenland.com) for more info.

World of Greenland (w worldofgreenland.com) For a more bespoke experience, World of Greenland has three lodges in the Ilulissat area.

*◀ **1** A TreeHouse Suite at the Arctic Treehouse Hotel. **2** Hotel Iso-Syöte's Eagle Suite has a tree growing through its centre. **3** Husky sledding at Star Arctic Hotel. **4** One of SnowCastle's sub-zero rooms.*

Location is key for each, and the company aims to take visitors off the beaten track – in comfort, of course. **Igloo Lodge** is its winter lodge, situated 15km out of Ilulissat. There are no roads leading here – you'll be transported by snowmobile or snowcat. Daytime activities include snowshoe hiking to an Icefjord viewpoint and to the Jakobshavn Glacier. Accommodation is either in igloos or in a bedroom in the heated cabin.

Glacier Lodge Eqi and **Ilimanaq Lodge** are open from mid-June to mid-September, so if you want to combine a trip with the northern lights, you'll have to book at the end of the season. Glacier Lodge Eqi sits about 80km north of Ilulissat and can be reached only by boat or helicopter. Its cabins overlook the Eqi Glacier, the most frequently calving glacier in the northern hemisphere – it's reckoned to calve about every 10 minutes. The Ilimanaq Lodge sits a boat ride away from Ilulissat – you'll need to zigzag through the icebergs of the Icefjord to get there. It is home to KOKS, a restaurant originally from the Faroe Islands where it has won two Michelin stars for its tasting menus. World of Greenland also specialises in excursions by helicopter, boat, dogsled and foot in the Ilulissat area.

ICELAND

Hotel Húsafell (w husafell.com) Less than 2 hours' drive from Reykjavik, contemporary Hotel Húsafell lies at the foot of the magnificent Borgarfjörður mountain range, whose peaks help to create those cloudless nights so cherished by aurora seekers. They see the northern lights about three times a week here during the winter months. When you're not standing with your head turned towards the heavens, there's ice caving, lava caving, hiking and lots of possibilities for lounging about in geothermal pools. You can swim, visit the Húsafell Canyon Baths in their rugged mountain setting, or take a dip in the Kruma Baths at Deildartunguhver.

Hotel Rangá (w hotelranga.is) Hotel Rangá's rural location means that no light pollution interferes with your aurora viewing; it enjoys vast open skies with 360° views, with mountains, glaciers and volcanoes providing a distant backdrop. Guests can lie back and watch the aurora from the hotel's naturally heated outdoor hot tubs and, if requested, staff will wake you during the night when the lights appear, so there's no need to wait rubbing your eyes into the small hours. There's also an observatory whose roof

1 Glacier Lodge Eqi overlooks the most frequently calving glacier in the northern hemisphere. 2 Igloo Lodge is accessible only by snowmobile. 3 Ilimanaq Lodge's restaurant, KOKS, has two Michelin stars at its original incarnation in the Faroe Islands. 4 Ice caving at Hotel Húsafell. ▶

MADS PIHL/VISIT GREENLAND

LUKE STACKPOOLE

SIMON BAJADA

HOTEL HÚSAFELL

At Eliassen Rorbuer, you can stay in one of the red-painted rorbuer for which the Lofoten Islands are famous

WERONIKA TROJANOWSKA (WWW.WERONIKATROJANOWSKA.PL)

retracts at the push of a button. It has two telescopes and on clear nights a local astronomer takes visitors on guided tours of the night sky.

For volcano enthusiasts, the hotel sits in the so-called Ring of Fire, where geothermal activity merrily spurts and bubbles. It is possible to take a sightseeing flight from here, weather permitting, as well as 4x4 excursions exploring the many places of interest in the area. The hotel is close to Skogafoss and Seljalandsfoss, two of Iceland's iconic waterfalls. The Golden Circle area is within easy reach, where visitors can tour spouting geysers, volcanic rifts and another waterfall, two-tiered Gullfoss, which sometimes freezes spectacularly in winter. For a longer day trip, Jökulsárlón glacier lagoon is filled with icebergs jostling for position as they head out to sea.

Hotel Sigló (w keahotels.is/siglo-hotel) This is a contemporary hotel in a historic spot, right on the waterfront in Siglufjörður, once a tiny shark-fishing village and a herring hot spot. Now the herring have gone, but the town still relies on the daily catch, which you can watch being brought in and then eat at any of the three restaurants in the Marina Village. The northern lights have a particularly scenic backdrop here – the town is squeezed between mountains and a narrow fjord on Iceland's north coast – and the hotel's hot tubs will keep your toes toasty as you stare into the skies. There's a microbrewery in the town, too.

NORWAY

Eliassen Rorbuer (w rorbuer.no) *Rorbuer* are the traditional, red-painted fishermen's huts for which the Lofoten Islands are famous. At Eliassen Rorbuer, the huts have been renovated as tourist cottages and sit right on the waterfront. Cottages have one or two bedrooms as well as kitchens, living and dining rooms, and there's a restaurant if you can't face cooking for yourself. You can take trips out to a spot with no light pollution if you want to see the northern lights. Ski touring is also available in winter.

SnowHotel Kirkenes (w snowhotelkirkenes.com) This snow hotel is in Kirkenes, right up Finland's northern coast, bordering Russia. As with other snow and ice hotels, it has a 'Snowhotel 365' meaning that you stay sub-zero year-round. Accommodation options include cold rooms with snow carvings, or northern lights cabins with panoramic windows. A unique attraction of the Kirkenes SnowHotel is its dog yard, one of the largest husky kennels in Norway with some 180 Alaskan huskies. Visitors can meet the dogs, play with the puppies when they have them, and take a sled ride. There are also reindeer here, and you can fish king crabs from the fjord. The Borderland Museum in Kirkenes is also worth a visit for its war exhibition: Kirkenes was a base for German forces in World War II and a target for Allied bombers.

SWEDEN

Abisko Mountain Station Abisko is reckoned to be one of the best places in the world to see the northern lights owing to its frequent clear skies and scant light pollution. The hotel here is the only one within the Abisko National Park. It's plain but comfortable (there are private bathrooms), and there's a restaurant, bar, small library and saunas. Self-catering accommodation and a campsite are also on offer, and you can take the chairlift directly up to Aurora Sky Station (page 35).

Arctic Bath (w arcticbath.se) This place takes the spa experience to a whole new level – even your cabin floats, in this case, on the Lule River in Swedish Lapland. The floating water cabins bob on the river's surface in summer, or are frozen into the ice in winter. For those who prefer to keep their feet on dry land, there are also land cabins and suites. Spa facilities (saunas, steam room, jacuzzis, cold pool) are available to all guests, and there's a full range of treatments you can book. Cosmetics and products are made by local therapists Care of Gerd (w careofgerd.se) using Swedish Lapland herbs and berries while the restaurant, too, has a focus on sustainable Scandinavian fare. Daytime activities include fishing, hiking, skiing at nearby Storklinten, and visits to a Sámi camp.

Brändön Lodge and Pine Bay Lodge (w brandonlodgelapland.com) These sister hotels are located on the Bay of Bothnia. Brändön is the main lodge, whose wooden cabins look out to sea; the hotel's snowmobile tours across the frozen sea ice and islands of the Luleå archipelago are particularly popular in winter, as are the resident reindeer. There are additionally dog-sled tours and all manner of northern lights experiences on offer. Pine Bay is more remote and more exclusive, with just nine rooms and a family cabin.

ICEHOTEL (w icehotel.com) When Yngve Bergqvist first came up with the idea of building a hotel entirely from ice in northern Sweden, everyone said he was barmy. Who on earth would want to sleep in a hotel made from ice, his incredulous friends and associates asked. The bank managers, meanwhile, stared glacially from behind their orderly Scandinavian spreadsheets and uttered a stark 'Nej'.

There was little funding. And so, in the late 1980s, the ICEHOTEL started small. Over the years, however, it's snowballed: there's a permanent ice bar in Stockholm and pop-up ice bars have been constructed from

At Arctic Bath the cabins float on the Lule River.

ARCTIC BATH

KIRUNA: A TOWN ON THE MOVE

There's something extraordinary about the Swedish town of Kiruna – the nearest town to the ICEHOTEL. Firstly, it's home to the LKAB mine, the largest iron-ore mine in the world, which has a staggering 400km of paved, two-lane underground roads and every day excavates sufficient iron ore to build six Eiffel Towers. But the most amazing thing about Kiruna is not the size of its mine, nor the fact that the expansion of the mine is putting the town at risk of sinking. No, the most surprising thing about this chilly town, 200km above the Arctic Circle, is that they're not mitigating the risk by closing the mine. Instead, they're moving the town.

By 2035, about a third of the town and 6,000 of its inhabitants will have relocated 3km to the east. The residents don't seem too fussed. After all, the town only exists because of the mine, which for more than 100 years has been the major employer in these parts. Still, it's a gargantuan task: schools, houses, hotels, office space, leisure facilities, hospitals and the rest must all be created. The new town looks very different to its former incarnation. Narrow streets are designed to help preserve the buildings' heat in Kiruna's sub-zero winters, while straight boulevards hope to channel the glacial winds.

Parts of the town have already made the move. The new shopping district opened in autumn 2022. Some buildings are brand-new architectural masterpieces, such as the town hall that opened in 2018. Known as The Crystal, it draws inspiration from the shape of iron minerals and incorporates the historic bell tower of its predecessor. The new town will be more sustainable than the old, with 90% of its heat production coming from residual heat from the mine rather than from biofuels; it will also generate wind energy.

Tokyo to Shanghai, Qingdao, Milan and Istanbul. At Jukkasjärvi, where the ICEHOTEL was born, there are now two ICEHOTELS: ICEHOTEL 365, which is open year-round and refrigerated by solar power from the midnight sun, and the winter-only ICEHOTEL, which is rebuilt each year by different artists with unique designs. There's also a whole village of warm facilities including accommodation and restaurants, a lounge and champagne bar in which the chilly visitor can take respite.

But it's still the sub-zero section of the ICEHOTEL that takes the breath away. The ice from the Torne River, from which the hotels are built – and back into which the winter ICEHOTEL gracefully melts each spring – is known for its purity and clarity. It's said to be better to drink than bottled mineral water. Maybe it's this, together with clever use of lighting, that makes this magnificent place more art gallery than hotel. Around 30,000

Kiruna's historic church will be moved in its entirety. An ornate wooden construction, it was once voted the best-loved building in the whole of Sweden. All 600 tonnes of it will be relocated in one go – and for this to happen, the roads will be widened and a railway viaduct demolished.

TOMMY ALVEN/S

Kiruna's historic church will move with the rest of the town.

litres of water are used in the construction of the winter hotel – that's 700 million snowballs to those whose minds can stretch to such a thing. The chandeliers alone comprise more than 1,000 hand-polished ice crystals. In the Icebar, even the glasses are made from ice – they'll slip from your hands if you're not wearing gloves. But unlike an ice cube, they're kept at a temperature just warm enough that they don't stick to your lips. Rather, the glass gently melts as you drink, moulding itself to the shape of your mouth.

Temperatures hover around –5°C in the standard ice rooms, where you sleep in thick sleeping bags on reindeer skins and a mattress on top of a wooden slatted base that slots into the ice-carved bedframe. These rooms are almost monastic in their simplicity, and utterly silent between their thick snow walls. But step across the hallway, through the avenue of glistening sculptures, and you'll come to the Art Suites. Here, individual artists from

1

TREEHOTEL

2

ASAF KLIGER/ICEHOTEL

countries across the world have each designed and created a bedroom. They're different every year. When I visited, there was a thrusting tango suite from Argentina, red-hot and sultry despite the ice, a delicate Japanese garden whose tiny details blended with the muted white tones, and Maori *moko* carved out of the ice by their Kiwi creator.

In ICEHOTEL 365, you choose between an Art Suite or one of nine Deluxe Suites, all of which have a bathroom. Some also come equipped with a sauna. And in summer? The ICEHOTEL harnesses the energy of the midnight sun. Power generated by solar panels keeps the hotel cool while its roof is insulated by grass and Arctic flowers.

Treehotel (w treehotel.se) Here's one for those who like their head in the clouds. Located by the Lule River near Harads, tree rooms hang several metres above ground level and are accessed via ramps and bridges. Treehouses they might be, but uncomfortable they're not – you get electricity, underfloor heating, a fridge and a toilet, though from most rooms you need to go back to ground if you want a shower. A recent addition is the Biosphere room whose façade contains 350 bird nests so that guests can become immersed in the bird life of the forest. There's also a roof terrace – and the Biosphere has its own shower and sauna. When you're done with birdwatching, there are snowmobile safaris, snowshoeing, cross-country skiing and, of course, watching out for the aurora.

◀**1** *Treehotel's treehouses are a slice of luxury.* **2** *ICEHOTEL is world renowned for its sub-zero rooms.*

5

The Northern Lights in History

EXPLORERS AND THE AURORA

In 1815, the Napoleonic Wars came to an end with the Battle of Waterloo. For the last few decades, officers of the British Navy had been gainfully employed trying to blast the French and the Americans off the face of the ocean; now that hostilities had ended, the Navy found itself with a surplus of officers who had to be retained on half pay. **John Barrow**, Second Secretary to the Admiralty, was blessed with a yearning for exploration – as well as a burning desire to do something useful with his surplus of men. He therefore rolled out his maps and set himself the task of filling in the blanks.

So began a great era of discovery. Barrow sent expeditions into the heart of Africa and to Antarctica (for more information read the excellent *Barrow's Boys* by Fergus Fleming – page 93), and he dispatched officers to the northern extremes of the globe: two of his missions were to find a trade route through the Northwest Passage, and to determine what lay at the North Pole. The naval officers heading these voyages were educated men. As they travelled they mapped coastlines, took scientific measurements and recorded their observations. Their experiences and theories relating to the northern lights added greatly to contemporary understanding of the phenomenon.

John Franklin – famous mainly for disappearing into the icy white, although his mapping of the North American coastline was a significant achievement – confirmed that appearances of the aurora were connected to magnetic activity. 'My opinion recorded in my former Narrative, that the different positions of the Aurora have a considerable influence upon the direction of the Magnetic Needle, has been repeatedly confirmed during our residence at Bear Lake. It was also remarked, that, from whatever point the flow of light, or, in other words, the motion of the Aurora proceeded, if that motion was rapid, the nearest end of the needle was drawn towards that point almost simultaneously with the commencement of the motion', Franklin wrote in his *Narrative of a Second Expedition to the Shores of the Polar Sea in the Years 1825, 1826 and 1827.*

After Barrow and his fur-clad missionaries passed on, a new generation of explorers followed in their wake, still puzzling over the same geographic conundrums. The Norwegian scientist and explorer **Fridtjof Nansen** was the first man to cross Greenland by ski; then in 1893 he sailed to the Arctic aboard the *Fram* and reached the highest latitude of any explorer yet, at 86°14'N. Nansen wrote lyrically about his observations of the northern lights. 'However often we see this weird play of light, we never tire of gazing at it', he wrote in his journal on 22 December 1895; he later published his account in a book titled *Farthest North.*

> It seems to cast a spell over both sight and sense till it is impossible to tear oneself away. It begins to dawn with a pale, yellow, spectral light behind the mountain to the east, like a reflection of a fire far away. It broadens, and soon the whole of the eastern sky is one glowing mass of fire. Now it fades again... After a while, scattered rays suddenly shoot up from the fiery mist, almost reaching to the zenith; then more; they play over the belt in a wild chase from east to west. They seem to be always darting nearer from a long, long way off. But suddenly a perfect veil of rays showers from the zenith out over the northern sky; they are so fine and bright, like the finest of glittering silver threads.

In 1905, Nansen's compatriot **Roald Amundsen** was the first man to succeed in negotiating the Northwest Passage; six years later he was also the first to reach the South Pole. He, too, recorded his observations of the aurora – and he was convinced that he heard them, as he wrote in his book *The South Pole.*

> The light is so wonderful; what causes this strange glow? ... It is one of the few really intense appearances of the aurora australis that receives us now. It looks as though Nature wished to honour our guests, and to show herself in her best attire. And it is a gorgeous dress she has chosen. Perfectly calm, clear with a starry sparkle, and not a sound in any direction. But wait: what is that? Like a stream of fire the light shoots across the sky, and a whistling sound follows the movement. Hush! Can't you hear? It shoots forward again, takes the form of a band, and glows in rays of red and green. It stands still for a moment, thinking of what direction it shall take, and then away again, followed by an intermittent whistling sound. So Nature has offered us on this wonderful morning one of her most mysterious, most incomprehensible, phenomena – the audible southern light.

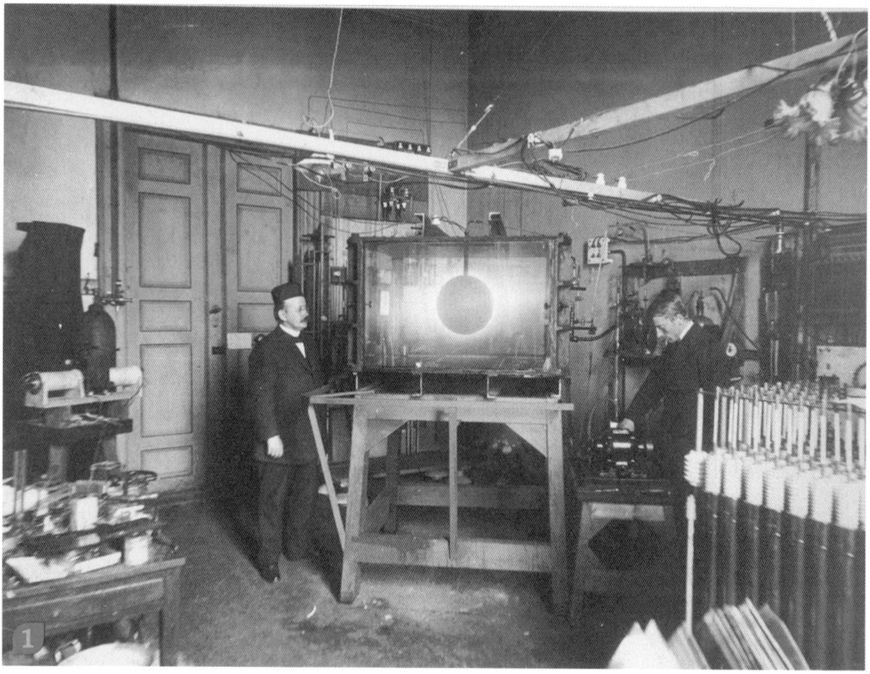

OLAF DEVIK/WC

SS

GODOT13/WC

SS

KRISTIAN BIRKELAND

Kristian Birkeland was the first man to claim that the aurora's source is the Sun. He correctly insisted that the Earth is surrounded by magnetic fields, which guide solar particles to the polar regions, where they produce light in the form of the aurora in the Earth's high atmosphere.

A bald, bespectacled man physically weakened by overwork and insomnia, Birkeland was born in Christiania (now Oslo) in Norway in 1867. Obsessed with auroral observation, he spent the winter of 1899–1900 cooped up in a specially built observatory on Haldde Mountain in the far north of Norway. When he wasn't being buffeted by frigid storms, he took ceaseless magnetic recordings of the aurora, and concluded that it is caused by electric currents in the Earth's high atmosphere that emanate from the Sun and are directed towards the polar regions; that these currents run at least 100km above the Earth's surface; and that magnetic disturbance is a result of these electric currents rather than a direct cause of the northern lights.

When Birkeland's leadership of a second research expedition to Russia was delayed by a dog bite and the need to recuperate from the side effects of a rabies vaccination, Birkeland used his enforced period of rest to think further about the aurora. He became convinced that, to fully understand it, he must recreate the aurora in laboratory conditions; this way he could be free not only from the risks posed by bad-tempered dogs but from the inconveniences of the Arctic weather.

His problem was money: the laboratory would cost more than he could possibly raise through his normal channels of funding. And so he tried his brain at business. He invented an electromagnetic cannon that, he claimed, would be able to fire from a ship further and faster than any weapon before. Unfortunately, the much-vaunted public unveiling of Birkeland's cannon was a disaster. His current short-circuited with a burst of flame and a fearsome roar, and shot an arc of brilliant white light across the auditorium from which some of the terrified audience fled. It also left a strange smell in the air, a bit like that which lingers after a lightning flash.

Plans for the cannon were off, but its dramatic failure gave Birkeland a new idea. The smell – created both by the faulty cannon and by lightning – was that of nitrogen oxidising. If Birkeland could reproduce the reaction, it would effectively mean he could manufacture lightning – and the nitrogen–

◀ **1** *Kristian Birkeland conducting his 'terrella' experiment.* **2** *Fridtjof Nansen saw the northern lights on his famous trip to the Arctic aboard the* Fram. **3** *A bust of Roald Amundsen in Svalbard.* **4** *Kristian Birkeland is honoured on the Norwegian 200-krone banknote.*

oxygen blend it produced would allow him to create fertiliser (a nitrogen–oxygen combination) on an industrial scale.

For three years Birkeland spent every waking minute working on a furnace to produce fertiliser. Then he sold his business interests and was free to work on his auroral theory. He built a vacuum tube, which he called a 'terrella'. Inside was a ball – standing in for the Earth – whose magnetism he could turn on and off. With conditions inside the tube created to mimic the Earth in space, he flooded the tube with electrons from a cathode. When he switched on the magnet, the electrons ran towards the 'Earth's' polar areas, and created rings – like the auroral ovals – around its magnetic north and south.

With his experiment, Birkeland demonstrated his idea that charged solar particles are directed by the Earth's magnetic field, which is comet-shaped with a tail tapering from the night-time side of the Earth, and that it's this that creates the northern lights. His work was so significant to astronomy that even today a portrait of Birkeland and a depiction of his 'terrella' illustrate Norway's 200-krone banknote, and the term 'Birkeland current' is still used to describe this particular field-aligned current.

But, just as it had made him, Birkeland's genius finished him. His marriage to the long-suffering Ida lasted six years; he was frequently absent due to work and, consumed by loneliness, she finally left him. An inveterate insomniac, Birkeland became addicted to the barbiturate veronal, which induced paranoia: towards the end of his life he became convinced that British spies were trying to steal his cannon invention, and ultimately that they wanted to kill him. He dismissed his domestic staff in case they might connive. He drank heavily. He travelled to Egypt and then to Japan where he worked hard, then feverishly, locking himself in his hotel room for weeks. On the morning of 15 June 1917 hotel staff found Birkeland dead. A postmortem concluded that he had taken 20 times the recommended dose of veronal. He was just 49.

GREAT AURORAS IN HISTORY

12 SEPTEMBER 1621 This was the show that gave the northern lights their name. Exactly which scientist – Galileo or Gassendi – was responsible for the term 'aurora borealis' may be open to debate (page 11). The intensity of the event that inspired them is not: this aurora was powerful enough to be seen as far south as France and Italy.

6 MARCH 1716 The great aurora of spring 1716 was observed by British astronomer Sir Edmund Halley; his decades-long desire to see a display of the aurora borealis was not rewarded until he was 60 years old. Halley was

MYTHS AND LEGENDS

Before the likes of Halley and Birkeland came along with their magnetic fields and their solar flares, the indigenous people of the north attributed all manner of powers and causes to the northern lights.

- Stories of warfare are often connected to the northern lights. Norse legend says that the lights are the glinting shields of Valkyrie warriors carrying their slain enemies to Valhalla, the hall of the dead, while intense displays of the aurora in southern Europe – where they are seen as blood-red – have been considered to be ominous portents of war.
- The aurora is widely connected to the game of football in Inuit legend. Some stories relate that the lights are a manifestation of human spirits playing football with a walrus head; others say that walrus spirits are playing the game with a human skull. Some even reckon that they're using the heads of naughty children. Certain Inuit people used to rush indoors when they saw the lights, terrified the aurora would slice off their heads to use as a new ball. Others carried knives to protect themselves from the wrathful spirits.
- Many legends attribute the northern lights to the spirits of the dead. In Iceland, it was believed that the spirits were trying to contact their living relatives, while in northern Canada they used to say that the lights were the spirits dancing to while away the long dark winter, and the colours were their festive clothing.
- It used to be commonly believed that you could bring on the aurora by whistling to it, and that clapping would stop the show. Some northerners thought that whistling or singing to the aurora was dangerous, however, as it enraged the spirits who might then sweep down to Earth and exact their revenge.
- The English legend of St George and the dragon is thought to have originated with the aurora, and many people believe that Chinese dragon legends, too, were born following ancient displays of the northern lights.

asked by the Royal Society to write up his observations in its publication *Philosophical Transactions*. This was the first detailed description of the aurora. Halley wrote, 'Auroral rays are due to the particles which are affected by the magnetic field; the rays are parallel to Earth's magnetic field.' Halley also correctly theorised that the corona form of the aurora was an

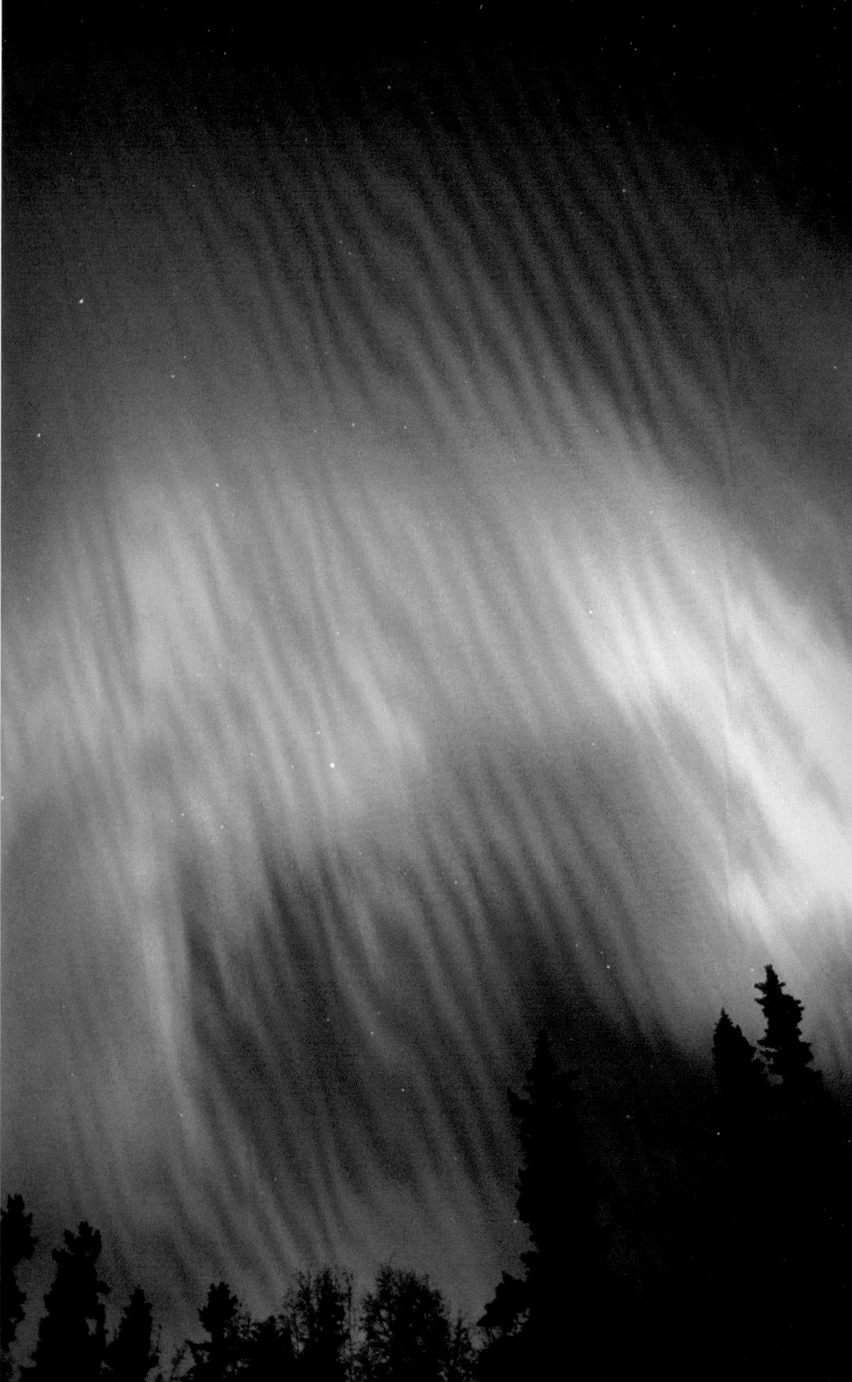

KEVIN SCHAFER/A

effect of perspective. He didn't hit on the source of the aurora, however – he surmised that luminous matter inside the Earth was escaping through cracks in its surface.

1–2 SEPTEMBER 1859 Tremendous solar flares shot out from the Sun in August and September 1859. They created the greatest space storms in recorded history. The plasma contained particularly intense magnetic fields and travelled at exceptionally high speeds – it's thought that the second eruption took just over 17 hours to reach the Earth, compared with the usual two to three days. The resulting aurora was seen as far south as Hawaii. Electrical surges disrupted telegraph lines across the northern United States and Canada; the current was so strong that the line between Portland and Boston ran for two hours without batteries, using the power of the aurora alone.

25 JANUARY 1938 'A remarkable and very beautiful appearance of the Aurora Borealis, or Northern Lights, was seen last night from many parts of England, including the South, where the spectacle is seldom to be seen', *The Times* reported from London. 'A Deal fisherman who returned to port last night said: "It appeared as if the whole heavens were on fire, and great beams of red light like steps stretched across the sky."' In Austria, some villagers called out the fire brigade to put out the supposed fires, while in Switzerland the Basel fire brigade was kept on stand-by as it was assumed the light came from fires in neighbouring Alsatian villages. Another *Times* journalist wrote, 'At Zeebrugge the sky was lighted up as if by a huge Bengal flare, and columns of light were seen rising from the sea as if from powerful projectors. The colour changed from red with white columns to blue, and a few seconds after the light had disappeared a large arc was seen over the town.'

13–14 MARCH 1989 This auroral display delivered such intense currents that in Québec, Canada, the power grid tripped, leaving six million people without electricity for nine hours. Magnificent displays were also observed across Europe.

28–29 OCTOBER 2003 Nicknamed the 'Halloween solar storm', this one overwhelmed the sensors that were measuring it. The aurora was seen as far south as Florida and the Mediterranean. Aircraft had to reroute from

◀ *During the 2003 'Halloween solar storm', the aurora was seen as far south as Florida and the Mediterranean.*

high altitudes near the Poles, and there was a power outage in Sweden for around an hour.

23 JULY 2012 Scientists compare this solar eruption to the 1–2 September event of 1859. Had it hit Earth, they believe the damage would have run into trillions of dollars. The good news was that it missed us by a week. Still, there was massive activity among the northern lights, with the aurora viewed in Cuba among other southerly locations.

Further Information

BOOKS

Bone, Neil *The Aurora: Sun–Earth Interactions* John Wiley & Sons, 1996. Bone delves deep into the mysterious world of physics, but his book is nonetheless comprehensible to non-scientists. It's detailed and useful for those who want to take their understanding to a higher level.

Davis, Neil *The Aurora Watcher's Handbook* Chicago University Press, 1992. This has a North American slant and was written back in the 1990s, but even for European readers it's probably still the best guide for the layperson wanting a detailed but accessible explanation.

Falck-Ytter, Harald *Aurora: The Northern Lights in Mythology, History and Science* Floris Books, 1999. Falck-Ytter's book is a straightforward read. As the title suggests, it covers legend and history as well as science.

Fleming, Fergus *Barrow's Boys* Granta Books, 2001. This doesn't really have anything to do with the northern lights, but for anyone interested in the exploration of northern parts, including the races for the Northwest Passage and the North Pole, this book makes riveting reading.

Jago, Lucy *The Northern Lights: How One Man Sacrificed Love, Happiness and Sanity to Solve the Mystery of the Aurora Borealis* Penguin Books, 2002. A meticulously researched and highly readable biography of Kristian Birkeland, the Norwegian scientist whose lifelong obsession with the aurora resulted in a greatly increased understanding of both the northern lights and of space.

Salisbury, Gay and Laney *The Cruellest Miles* Bloomsbury, 2003. Again, nothing to do with the aurora, but this is a fabulous account of the 1925 serum run, in memory of which the Iditarod race is run.

WEBSITES

SOHO (Solar and Heliospheric Observatory) is a space-borne observatory operated by the ESA (European Space Agency) in collaboration with NASA. Even if you don't harbour a deep fascination for the inner workings of the Sun, SOHO's website (w soho.nascom.nasa.gov) is worth a visit for its incredible images.

The **University of Alaska Fairbanks Geophysical Institute** has an excellent website. Go to its aurora forecast page (w gi.alaska.edu/AuroraForecast), which includes the forecast for all auroral regions. Click on the links for further information on the northern lights – the FAQ page is particularly helpful. You can also sign up for email alerts from the Geophysical Institute that will tell you when auroral activity in your area is predicted to be high.

Another great website for updates on auroral displays is w spaceweather.com. Alongside northern lights updates and links to NASA there's also an area where you can submit your own photos of the display. Last but not least, the **British Astronomical Association** (Britain's leading association for the amateur astronomer) has an auroral section on its website with useful tips for observing and photographing the lights, and well-laid-out info on the science behind the aurora (w britastro.org/sections/aurora-nlc).

INDEX OF ADVERTISERS

A musher's perspective. ▶

ANINGAAQ ROSING CARLSEN/VISIT GREENLAND

THE BRADT STORY

In the beginning

It all began in 1974 on an Amazon river barge. During an 18-month trip through South America, two adventurous young backpackers – Hilary Bradt and her then husband, George – decided to write about the hiking trails they had discovered through the Andes. *Backpacking Along Ancient Ways in Peru and Bolivia* included the very first descriptions of the Inca Trail. It was the start of a colourful journey to becoming one of the best-loved travel publishers in the world; you can read the full story on our website (bradtguides.com/ourstory).

Getting there first

Hilary quickly gained a reputation for being a true travel pioneer, and in the 1980s she started to focus on guides to places overlooked by other publishers. The Bradt Guides list became a roll call of guidebook 'firsts'. We published the first guide to Madagascar, followed by Mauritius, Czechoslovakia and Vietnam. The 1990s saw the beginning of our extensive coverage of Africa: Tanzania, Uganda, South Africa, and Eritrea. Later, post-conflict guides became a feature: Rwanda, Mozambique, Angola, and Sierra Leone, as well as the first standalone guides to the Baltic States following the fall of the Iron Curtain, and the first post-war guides to Bosnia, Kosovo and Albania.

Comprehensive – and with a conscience

Today, we are the world's largest independently owned travel publisher, with more than 200 titles. However, our ethos remains unchanged. Hilary is still keenly involved, and **we still get there first**: two-thirds of Bradt guides have no direct competition.

But we don't just get there first. Our guides are also known for being **more comprehensive** than any other series. We avoid templates and tick-lists. Each guide is a one-of-a-kind expression of an expert author's interests, knowledge and enthusiasm for telling it how it really is.

And a commitment to wildlife, conservation and respect for local communities has always been at the heart of our books. Bradt Guides was **championing sustainable travel** before any other guidebook publisher. We even have a series dedicated to Slow Travel in the UK, award-winning books that explore the country with a passion and depth you'll find nowhere else.

Thank you!

We can only do what we do because of the support of readers like you – people who value less-obvious experiences, less-visited places and a more thoughtful approach to travel. Those who, like us, take travel seriously.